David Torkington's Trilogy
on Prayer comprises

The Hermit
The Prophet
The Mystic

To Bobby

Without whose encouragement, help, and advice
this book could not have been written.

The Mystic

From Charismatic to Mystical Prayer

DAVID TORKINGTON

ALBA·HOUSE   NEW·YORK

SOCIETY OF ST. PAUL, 2187 VICTORY BLVD., STATEN ISLAND, NEW YORK 10314

ST PAULS

Library of Congress Cataloging-in-Publication Data

Torkington, David.
    The Mystic: from charismatic to mystical prayer / David Torkington.
       p. cm.
    Sequels to final part of a trilogy: The hermit and The prophet.
    ISBN 0-8189-0852-1
    I. Title.
    PR6070.0657M97   1999
    823'.914 — dc21   98-32161
                                          CIP

Produced and designed in the United States of America by the
Fathers and Brothers of the Society of St. Paul,
2187 Victory Boulevard, Staten Island, New York 10314,
as part of their communications apostolate.

Published in the United States of America by special arrangement
with Mercier Press, Cork, Ireland.
    ISBN 0-8189-0850-5 — The Hermit
    ISBN 0-8189-0851-3 — The Prophet
    ISBN 0-8189-0852-1 — The Mystic
    ISBN 0-8189-0859-9 — 3-Volume Trilogy on Prayer

Printing Information:

Current Printing - first digit   1   2   3   4   5   6   7   8   9   10

Year of Current Printing - first year shown

1999   2000   2001   2002   2003   2004   2005   2006   2007

1

If there's one particular animal that I can't abide, it's the road-hog. It's quite capable of annoying me at the best of times, but at the worst of times when it's sniffing and snorting behind me on the motorway I become quite uncontrollable. The human in me simply snaps, and the beast bursts out making me quite capable of anything.

Only last March I was on the way to a funeral in Manchester when I thought I saw one of those animals closing up on me with reckless speed.

It was one of those rare mornings when the milk of human kindness was flowing so freely through my veins that I was actually preparing to vacate the fast lane to allow him through, charitably assuming that his need was greater than mine, when — would you believe it? — he started flashing his lights at me!

That did it. The milk of human kindness suddenly soured, and I refused to give way.

I couldn't believe my ears when I first heard him hooting at me, but it went on and on with the insistent bark of a machine gun. I looked at my speedometer. I was doing over eighty-five miles an hour. Wasn't that enough for him?

I'd borrowed a friend's Jag for the week, so I decided to give him a run for his money and accelerated to over a hundred, but the maniac accelerated with me. It was the first time I'd driven over a hundred and I was beginning to get scared; when he began flashing his lights and hooting his horn again, terror took hold of me and anger gave way to fear, so I pulled over to allow him through.

It was then that I noticed the red fluorescent stripe down the side of the car, saw the flashing blue light on the roof and then finally came face to face with a blue-coated lump of granite behind the wheel, that motioned me into the side of the road.

If it were a mere matter of breaking the speed limit I don't suppose I'd have been in such a state, but it was much more than that. So there I sat, trembling like a naughty schoolboy, waiting for the headmaster to call me into his study for the caning I only half deserved.

"What's all the hurry?" said the lump of granite when he finally emerged with a pencil and notebook at the ready.

He sounded almost human!

"So sorry, Officer," I said. "I'm in such a hurry to get to a funeral that I simply didn't see you."

"Whose funeral's so important that it makes you risk your own?" he said.

"It's my best friend's, or rather it's his mother's," I said, trying to gain some sort of composure.

He shook his head and aimed his pencil at the notebook.

"Name?"

"Peter Calvay."

"Occupation?"

"Well, I suppose you'll have to put down 'hermit,'" I said.

"Who's a hermit?" said the police officer, gaping at me incredulously.

"My friend," I said. "Peter Calvay."

"I don't mean him, I mean you!"

"Oh, sorry. My name's James Robertson. I'm a priest."

"Oh, I see!" he said, softening slightly. "And are you officiating at this funeral?"

It was a lifeline so I grabbed it.

"Oh yes. I'm the concelebrant," I said, hoping he didn't know precisely what that meant. "That's why I was in such a hurry. That's why I didn't see you."

"Well, I suppose that's a bit different," he said, scratching his head with the pencil, "but it's no excuse for speeding! Where is this funeral?"

"It's at Saint Catherine's, Didsbury, and it's due to start in half an hour!"

"Saint Catherine's, School Lane?" he said.

"That's it!"

"Right, get in your car and follow me!"

To this day I don't know how fast I went. It was simply too fast to even glance at the speedometer, but even then we arrived five minutes late.

Peter's younger brother, David, was officiating at the funeral. He was sitting down to listen to the first lesson as I took my place at the back of the church. I was too late to join him. It was Peter's father who read, with a clear full voice that belied the inner turmoil that must have been playing hell with his insides. His eldest son, Tony, followed him, reading a long responsorial psalm, then Peter read the second lesson. When the father and the two older brothers had taken their place again in the main body of the church, David read the Gospel and then began to preach about his mother.

It was remarkable how the father and the sons had voices that were almost identical, given a semitone here and a semitone there — fine voices too, rich and powerful. I wasn't surprised to learn from David's sermon that his family were all great talkers, but not, he admitted, great listeners. This was one of the reasons why his mother was so loved, because she knew how to listen.

David had obviously been very close to his mother. His words were charged with an extraordinary potency and power, precisely because he was trying so desperately to suppress the emotion that welled up from within. Tony was joined by his wife, Protasia, and his two young sons, Mark and Simon, to help him take the gifts up to the altar. The boys hadn't reached double figures yet and they were far too young to experience the sense of grief that enveloped the rest of the family. It was all too much for them — all they knew was that Uncle David, who'd recently been chasing them around the garden dressed as Dracula, had suddenly become all solemn and serious. Even Uncle David had to smile at the sheepish grins and the half smiles that his nephews gave him with the gifts they bore.

As he turned back from the altar, he reached out to take the wine and water from his brother and sister-in-law. The boys misinterpreted their uncle's movements, with disastrous consequences. They both screamed out aloud, thinking that he'd reverted to type, and ran squealing back to their places where they dissolved into fits of giggles. Even Grandad had to smile with the rest of the family — it wasn't the boys' fault. Nobody quite knew when to take Uncle David seriously, it seemed, least of all the boys.

I only stayed with the family for an hour or so after the funeral, but it was long enough to experience something of the loving care and support that would sustain Peter's father in the months ahead, when the numbness he felt at first would die down and the heartache would rise up and remain with him until the one he had lost was once again by his side, never to be lost again.

I went back to the presbytery where Peter had arranged for me to stay for a few days. I sat down in my room and reflected upon the various events that had brought me to seek out Peter for a third time.

I'd first met him on the Isle of Barra in the Outer Hebrides four years before, where I'd sought his help. He'd been living the life of a hermit for over twenty years.

I'd been so busy changing the world in those first years since my ordination that I had all but forgotten about the prayer life without which my pastoral work was doomed to failure. Peter had not only been able to put things in their true perspective, but he'd been able to give me the sort of practical help that I so desperately needed. I was shattered when in the following year I heard that he had been lost at sea and was presumed dead. The local parish priest had asked me to go through his things on Calvay, his island home, and inform his many correspondents of his untimely death. I'd hardly completed the first stage of my job when Peter turned up again, after spending several months in Russia. It seemed he'd had a heart attack in his own boat, and the Russian trawler that picked him up took him back to their homeland because they had strict orders not to put in to any foreign port.

Though I received further spiritual help from Peter, not least in my prayer life, Peter once again avoided the subject of mystical prayer when I mentioned the matter, as I had done on my first visit. He didn't in any way patronize me, but he made it quite clear that there would be time enough for us to discuss it when I was ready, but that was not yet. However, in the two years since my second visit to Peter, events had taken place in my own spiritual journey that led Peter to believe that the time was at last ripe for him to explain matters that he was reluctant to discuss with me earlier. But perhaps I'd better explain.

Since those two visits to him on Barra, I had scrupulously followed all that Peter had told me to do, making sure that I put aside what he called "quality space and time for prayer." I didn't give up any of my work or pastoral activities unless they prevented me from putting God first in this way each day.

After the initial difficulties through which Peter had helped me, everything seemed to get better and better, and my prayer time soon became an indispensable source of strength and consolation. A priest friend had introduced me to the charismatic movement and I used to go with him to a prayer group once a week. I was a bit skeptical to begin with, but when a group of fellow priests laid hands on me at a midweek retreat for the clergy, I threw away all my inhibitions and just let myself go. Somehow the Spirit seemed to take over. At all events, I no longer felt embarrassed about praying in public and even sharing with people with whom I had felt quite reticent before.

Peter seemed very interested in the charismatic movement when I wrote to tell him about it, though he frankly admitted he'd had no experience of group prayer at all. One thing he insisted upon very strongly indeed was that I kept up the daily time for personal prayer in private, come hell or high water, whether I felt like it or not.

During those two years my prayer life seemed to grow in leaps and bounds. Peter continued to advise and encourage me, but as things got better and better I corresponded with him less and less. He had actually said that as long as things were going well there would be no need to write so frequently. I have never been a good letter-writer, and since I felt my prayer life was going rather well — to put it modestly — I didn't feel the need for the sort of help that Peter had given me in the beginning.

My initial success at prayer, albeit with Peter's help, had given me a rather inflated idea of my own importance. Since my private prayer had become not only easier but full of sweetness and light, and since I seemed to have had all the inspirations in the prayer groups that I had led, I began to think that God was especially using me. I loved to guide and lead others and I gathered a group of followers about me who would come to my Masses and prayer groups. Everything seemed to be going fine, the sky was blue and there was not even a cloud on the horizon, save an occasional cynical stick-in-the-mud, who would make some smart-alec remark about emotionalism or the like. This always used to annoy me. Why did they feel they had to snipe at others just because they hadn't the humility to let themselves go, and open themselves to the Spirit? There were too many ecclesiastical stuffed shirts around who were all closed up in themselves and became sarcastic and waspish when they were confronted by others who just wanted to praise the Lord.

Then, something rather shattering happened last September. Just when I thought I was on the verge of a major spiritual breakthrough I had a spiritual breakdown instead, or so it seemed.

The prayer life that had meant so much to me in the last couple of years had reached a crescendo — it was almost too good to be true. Then the bubble burst, leaving me flat. I just didn't know what to do with myself. I continued to go to the prayer groups and gave the daily time for private prayer that Peter had insisted upon so emphatically, but something terrible had happened, and it seemed to have happened almost overnight.

I didn't write to Peter about it because I didn't know what to say, and I thought everything would right itself in a day or two, or a week or two at the most, but it didn't! I remember sending him a card at Christmas and scribbling a few lines, but I didn't write a proper letter because I couldn't. Words still failed me. I went over everything Peter had told me about prayer in the past, and I gave everything another chance. The blueprint for prayer that he had given me was no longer of any help. I tried to use the Scriptures in the way that I had become accustomed to using them, but they left me as dry as dust. Those especially prized passages that used to lift me out of myself into a sort of spiritual euphoria now left me absolutely cold. I tried some of my favorite poems. I tried the hymns that never failed to move me, but they moved me no more. The prayer time that had for so long been my little heaven on earth became my hell, as I battled for concentration and desperately tried to squeeze out some of the spiritual sweetness that I had experienced so often before.

I felt a fraud when I took part in the prayer groups, saying the same things I had always said, praying the same prayers, but knowing that they no longer came from my heart, but from my head. At first I justified myself with the thought that things would soon get back to normal, that my spiritual feelings would stir once more, but in the meantime I felt like a camel lost in the desert. I was living off a hump that was getting smaller with each passing day, and I knew I couldn't go on like that for much longer. By early spring I came to realize that I just couldn't go on. I not only felt that my prayer life was in danger but that even my faith was beginning to falter. It was at this point that I wrote the following desperate letter to Peter asking for his help.

Dear Peter,

Please excuse me for not writing to you for such a long time. It must be six months or more since you last heard from me. The truth of the matter is, I simply didn't know how to express myself.

Something terrible has happened and I don't know how to tell you about it. Until last September, everything was going according to plan. I really felt that I was getting somewhere at last in the spiritual life. Prayer had become easy to me after those early difficulties that you helped me through. A few words from my favorite Scripture passages were enough to engage my whole being throughout my prayer time, filling me with an exhilarating sense of God's presence and love.

My new-found spiritual energies spilled over into my work and especially into the prayer groups that I had founded and led. Then, unexpectedly, sometime in September, I seemed to be holed and my spiritual resources drained away. Almost overnight I found myself out in the cold, banished without rhyme or reason from the warm hearth that I was beginning to believe was my spiritual birthright. At first I thought it was merely some temporary setback and I would return once more to the cozy fireside. But as the months passed by, the cold was clothed with an ever-deepening darkness and I was assailed by hordes of marauding distractions that cut and thrust at my mind from within.

In spite of all this I kept up the daily time you had insisted I should give to prayer, though my heart was not in it. I must admit, quite frankly, that in recent weeks I have been finding excuse after excuse to escape from the prayer that was once my heaven but is now my hell.

I still lead the prayer groups, but I, who was once their mainspring and inspiration, feel like an outsider. The other members of the group must have noticed the change. A regular attender asked me only yesterday if I was feeling all right. Rather than admit that I was on the verge of losing my faith, I admitted to being a little out of sorts and promised to go to the doctor as soon as possible. But it is not the doctor I need. I feel sure you are the only one who can help me, Peter, though I don't know how. I feel I have come to the end of my tether and I don't know what to do with myself.

Please do excuse the rather dramatic and desperate tone of this letter, but it expresses no more than I feel. I do hope I will hear from you in the very near future.

With every good wish. Please pray for me!

James Robertson

Peter's reply came by return of post.

Dear James,

Thank you so much for your long-awaited letter. I had already guessed the predicament that you were in. Take it from me, everything has not ended — indeed, it is only beginning.

In short, you have just come through what is usually called first fervor. Everybody must go through this particular phase in their spiritual development if they are going to come to know and experience the fullness of love for which they crave.

There are four main stages in a person's prayer life, Juvenile Prayer, Adolescent Prayer, Adult Prayer and Perfect Prayer. At the Juvenile stage a person is very insecure and lacks confidence in themselves and in God, so they choose to live in a stable and secure world. It is the world of prescribed prayers learned by heart, or read from a book. It is the world of set formulas and well-tried devotional exercises.

The Adolescent stage follows if and when a believer decides to make their own the faith that they have imbibed with their mother's milk. The world of the adolescent is less predictable and more exciting. Sensing that God is calling them onwards they respond by searching for Him in an ever-deepening prayer experience. Fervor, spiritual cocksureness and pride characterize the make-up of the adolescent, though they are usually only aware of their fervor.

Traditionally, the prayer experience of the adolescent took place behind the closed and private doors of interior mental prayer.

In more recent years, many people have been passing through this stage in the company of others, as members of prayer groups. You have combined both.

The moment of truth comes when first fervor comes to an end and a believer finds themselves deprived of all feeling in their prayer life. It is sad to say, but the vast majority give up serious personal prayer at this point, because their most recent experience had conditioned them to associate faith with feelings, or the tangible awareness of God's Presence with His actual Presence. If they only knew it, God has just taken a new initiative and drawn them closer to Himself than ever before. However, this new, more spiritual Presence of God seems like absence to the adolescent whose previous experience of Him was almost entirely sensual. The days of adolescence are now over — never to return again. This is the beginning of Adult Prayer.

This new world in which a believer finds themselves is the environment that enables them to become adults, by daily learning to give without receiving and to love without feeling that love being returned. If you think about it, you will see that this is the only way a person can become a perfect lover. The love that is always returned in kind must remain for ever suspect until it receives nothing in return and yet goes on giving. This is the beginning of mystical prayer. The great spiritual writers make it quite clear that the beginner who perseveres will be stripped of all feeling and fervor, and will be given the opportunity of becoming a perfect and selfless lover. Naturally the "bounty-hunter" who is only looking for exciting and exhilarating experiences will pack up serious personal prayer altogether at this point.

Throughout the ages, Christian tradition has given various names to this painful period in the spiritual journey. For some it is the Desert, the Wilderness, for others it is the Cloud of Unknowing, the House of Self-Knowledge, the Prayer of Faith or the Dark Night of the Soul. All these different expressions are used by Christian tradition throughout the ages to convey the meaning and implications of the challenge with which the Gospel confronts a person who wants to become a perfect follower of Christ.

The challenge is this. Do you want to be identified with the full human being, the Perfect Adult who emerged from the tomb on the first Easter Day? Do you want to experience the fullness of love that Christ experienced in His resurrection, and share it with others? If so, then you must be prepared to share in His self-sacrificial life, in His death too, and even in His descent into hell! It means literally that!

Anyone can follow Christ when He is working miracles, turning water into wine and handing out free food and drink. It is not difficult to be His disciple when you can see Him curing the sick, giving back sight to the blind and even raising the dead. But how many can follow Him into the desert to suffer hunger, thirst, loneliness and temptation? How many are prepared to carry a cross behind Him, to follow Him to Calvary, to descend into the very bowels of evil with Him? Juveniles can't. Adolescents can't. It takes an adult to do that, or rather, an adolescent becomes an adult by doing that.

Well, that will have to do for now. I will write again soon because I have a lot to say to you. For the moment, keep up the daily quality time for prayer as you did before, and keep your heart's attention fixed upon God as best you can. Now is the time when you must learn to give without counting the cost, to love without receiving in return, so that your love may be strengthened and deepened in such a way that you may come to know and experience the height and the depth, the length and the breadth of God's love, which surpasses all our understanding.

With every good wish,

Peter

I put Peter's letter down and sat back to think over its implications. He certainly didn't beat about the bush. It was straightforward, clear and to the point. I knew what he was saying was right, although its implications wounded my pride.

Here was I, a priest in my mid-thirties, and I had only just passed through my first fervor. I began to look back briefly, with not a little embarrassment, on some of the brash and boisterous escapades of my spiritual adolescence. Yes, Peter had played down the truth so as not to over-embarrass me, but I could see how I had acted like a cocky teenager on so many occasions. Just because my prayer time had been filled with unction, I thought that I was about to scale Mount Carmel when I hadn't even penetrated the foothills at its base! I had thought I could trace my spiritual progress to the Seventh Mansion of Saint Teresa's *Interior Castle*, when I hadn't so much as crossed the drawbridge! I loved to read about the most lofty experiences of the Christian mystics and I had the arrogance to identify them with my own. I'd fancied myself as a spiritual guru and loved to advise and guide others. I mentally blushed as I thought of some of the patronizing advice I had given to others who had been journeying for years in the prayer of faith, the prayer without feeling, that I hadn't even known about until now.

In the last few months I had been deeply depressed at what appeared to be my failure in prayer and my weaknesses of character that were beginning to come to the surface. My continual temptation was to think I was wasting my time in prayer and I kept wanting to pack it all in and lose myself in my work. There, at least, I would be able to see my efforts rewarded by tangible success. My youth work alone could easily absorb all my energies and keep me off the lonely streets of my mind, where I seemed to loaf about aimlessly, doing nothing and getting nowhere in particular.

A priest to whom I used to go to confession had told me to get more fresh air, take up a hobby or throw myself into my work. "Whatever you do," he said, "get out of yourself." Come to think of it, I had given the same sort of advice to countless others in the past. If I couldn't turn them on to my prevailing spiritual exuberance, then I'd try to urge them to lose themselves in someone or something else. In many cases my advice might have been good and acceptable, but I knew there had been occasions when it was a cover-up operation to hide my own ignorance and to get rid of problem cases that I couldn't handle or just didn't interest me.

I began to see that countless would-be contemplatives must have been frustrated and positively misguided by the scandalous ignorance of the very people who ought to have been able to lead them and direct them. I was one of those people. If I couldn't be blamed in the past, then I could and would be blamed in the future if I didn't take full advantage of my friendship with Peter. Thank God for Peter. Even his brief letter gave me grounds for renewed confidence. It was quite evident that he knew what he was talking about.

I immediately wrote another letter thanking him for explaining so clearly my present predicament, and expressing my disappointment when I realized that at my age I was only just emerging out of spiritual adolescence. Peter's reply came a week later.

Dear James,

Thank you so much for your frank and honest reactions to my last letter. I didn't in any way mean to be offensive, and I do hope you haven't taken it that way. I was only explaining your present predicament as clearly as I could.

You see, spiritual adolescence has nothing to do with age. You might be in your thirties, your forties, your fifties or whatever, but you still have to pass through it if you want to enter into spiritual maturity. It is just the same with human psychological development. You can be psychologically a juvenile or an adolescent at any age. If a person is going to attain a relative degree of maturity, then they will have to pass through the preceding stages, no matter whether they be twenty-two or eighty-two. No one can become an adult without first passing through their adolescence.

I know that I have fobbed you off in the past when you have asked me about mystical prayer, but I only did this because I saw no point in discussing matters with you of which you had no experience. You have, whether you realize it or not, already experienced the beginnings of the mystic way and so I won't fob you off any longer; in fact, please be encouraged to come and see me as soon as possible. Would there be any chance of your coming out here for the second week in March? It would certainly suit me best. If not, let me know how you are fixed for time. I'm sure we can find a mutually acceptable date.

Every good wish,

Peter

All had been arranged for the second week in March when Peter's mother suddenly died. She'd had heart trouble for some time, but the end came with a suddenness that shocked everybody, not least Peter. She'd been in the middle of a conversation with her brother-in-law when her head suddenly fell forward and she died. Peter caught the morning plane that same day and arrived home to find his father in a terrible state. Both his brothers were tied up at the time so it fell to Peter to make all the necessary arrangements. He phoned me the next day to cancel our arrangements to meet on Barra, but he invited me to concelebrate with his younger brother David at the funeral the following Monday, and then stay on for a few days so that we could talk things over. I didn't want to overburden Peter at such a time so I told him to forget about our plans to meet until a later date but he was so insistent that I accepted.

I had just finished breakfast on the day after the funeral when I was called to the phone. It was Peter.

"How are you fixed for time this morning?"

"Fine!"

"I could come round in about twenty minutes?"

"Great, but are you sure it's all right?"

"Yes, no problem — my aunt and my cousin have just arrived and they're going to help Dad go through my mother's things. So, I'll see you soon!"

"Okay, I'll be waiting!"

2

"It's just like old times," I said to Peter, as I remembered the long conversations we'd had at North Bay on the Isle of Barra.

"Yes," said Peter, "it hardly seems four years since our first meeting."

Peter's chair creaked as his enormous frame crashed into its solar plexus.

"That's better!" he said. Then it came — that unforgettable and unique smile, that transformed an already handsome face into something quite other-worldly. I'd seen it so often before but it still captivated me, even more than the most unforgettable sunset I'd ever seen. It would make you believe in angels, if you'd never believed in them before. I mean middle-aged angels, of course, for Peter had already scaled the heights of his youth and was more than halfway down the other side. Something David had said in his sermon enabled even my soggy little computer to work out that Peter must be almost forty-five, though he didn't look it.

The few grey hairs that I had detected on our first meeting seemed to have disappeared — maybe it was the light, but his heavy crop of black hair appeared quite unreproachable, save for its length. It would henceforth be able to crawl unchallenged further and further down his back now that its only challenger had passed to her reward. It was a surprise to me to see Peter looking so well and hardly affected by his mother's death. True, he looked tired, but that was only to be expected — he'd had a lot to do since coming home. Maybe death doesn't affect you the same way when you've faith as strong as Peter's, I thought. After all, his mother had just arrived at the very place to which he himself was traveling with all the speed he could muster.

It took only two months to prove me wrong, two months before the terrible sense of loss that his present busyness kept at bay burst into his conscious mind to break him up and bring him down into a deep depression. I'd still so much to learn. I still believed that true sanctity produced disembodied spirits, men and women who had so freed themselves from the world of matter and form, of flesh and blood, that they could remain aloof from and untouched by the world to which the rest of us belong as they await their final consummation in the land of the Blessed Spirits.

Peter was to prove me wrong, not just by what he was to say to me, but by what he was to be to me, and what I was to see he was to others, who clearly saw in him a genuine embodiment of the Man he had committed himself to follow. True sanctity sensitizes the body and the soul in such a way that a person is fully open to receive the Spirit of God, who bonds them together into a harmonious wholeness that makes them more human than they ever were before. No one is more human than the saint, who is able to feel more fully for others than any other who has not felt the touch of the abiding Presence within him.

"I'm so sorry to drag you away from your family at such a time as this," I said.

"No need to apologize at all," said Peter. "Frankly, I do need a break from the tensions of the last few days. I've been with my poor dad almost night and day for the past week. He's in a terrible state though he's trying not to show it. It's all beginning to get to me."

"Well, Peter, I don't know where to begin."

"I know you don't," said Peter, smiling, "but I think *I* do. Your letters made everything clear to me, so I'll begin for you! To put it simply, you are at the beginning of what people used to call the mystic way, though you probably think that I am deceived. What

16

I want to do for you, before going any further, is to try and put everything into perspective. By everything, I mean the prayer journey to which you have undoubtedly committed yourself.

"If someone asks directions for a long and hazardous journey, it's a good idea to begin by mapping out the way ahead in its entirety, so that they can see at a glance the route they are to follow, before you begin to draw their attention to particular problems that you anticipate they will have to encounter upon their way.

"The difference in your case is that the journey that you have embarked upon is not to some place, but to some Person. It has begun, not because you have decided to make the journey, but because Someone has offered you an invitation to which you are responding. I'll explain more precisely how that invitation is received shortly, but for the moment let's concentrate on the nature of the prayer journey.

"The Old Testament, the New Testament, as well as the Fathers of the Church, all insist that the only way this journey can be understood properly is by paralleling it to the journey made by two lovers who commit themselves to one another for life.

"Now, the incredible thing is that although I've known this for many years, and have used this analogy often enough in helping other people along the way, I've only just come to understand it properly myself during the past week. But let me explain what I mean!

"Every morning before the funeral, my father woke me up with a cup of tea, sat on my bed, and began to tell me a story that I'd never heard before. It was a love story, it was the story of my father's love for my mother and her love for him, a story that spanned over fifty years. I found the whole story fascinating, not just because it was the tale of my own origins, but because it gave me a new and deeper insight into the spiritual journey; an insight that I had never had so clearly before.

"My father couldn't remember how it began. All he could remember was that they used to love playing together in primary school. The first time any words of affection had been passed between them was in the context of playing 'happy families,' in and around the garden shed. But these words soon took on a more significant meaning when they were first used outside play, on the way to and from school. This was the first phase of a love that was to develop into something far deeper later.

"The point I want to draw to your attention for the analogy is that, although seeds were sown that were reaped later, their love was hardly more than rudimentary. It was juvenile love. They certainly expressed their feelings for one another, but — and this is the point I want to make — there was no conformity between the words they used and the way they felt. No doubt there was some feeling there, but there was no conformity between the rather lavish language of love that they'd picked up from their parents or their older brothers or sisters, and the way they felt about each other inside. Circumstances similar to those that separated them at the end of their primary schooling drew them together again seven years later. Their relationship resumed, but this time the love that grew between them was quite different.

"The language once used in their childhood innocence was used again, but this time with heartfelt meaning that had never been felt by those children long ago, who'd played 'happy families' in the garden shed. Now for the first time, my father said, he experienced the true feelings that were meant to accompany the words used in his childhood innocence, feelings that became so strong, and on occasions so other-worldly, that no words he'd ever read, no phrases ever used before could describe the inexpressible feelings he had for his beloved Agnes.

"The union of minds and hearts was deepened by a union of bodies as they came closer and closer to one another in the early years of married love, when potent and powerful passions thrust them forward together upon a journey that would finally lead to the most perfect union of personalities possible here on earth. They were exciting and exhilarating, those days of adolescent love that bonded them ever more fully together before and after their wedding day.

"There were times, even then, when the most pure and passionate love-making would lead them both onwards to savor in silence what each had received from the other — in moments when they seemed to have passed beyond the world of flesh and blood to reach out to touch eternity. This is what I will call adolescent love for the sake of the analogy.

"Something happened, when everything was going so well, that my father has never been able to understand, something that changed their relationship. At the time, he was sure that it was for the worse, but later he came to see it was for the better, though it meant a lot of pain and suffering at the time.

"All my father could say was that the feelings, the emotions and passions that had been so powerful, gradually began to wane. It seemed to happen to my mother first, though later my father began to notice it happening to him. He said on reflection that it was as if they had been led on through, and beyond each other to an experience that made them feel dissatisfied with even the most magical moments of married love, because some other love seemed to beckon. It's a theme you find in many great novelists, like D.H. Lawrence, for instance, whose characters are always glimpsing the numinous through the other and hungering for a love that their partner is unable to satisfy completely.

"They'd both noticed a change in their relationship before James, my eldest brother, was born, so that wasn't the cause of it. But it did add to the difficulties both were experiencing in their relationship. My father humbly admitted that he felt my mother was giving too much of her love and attention to her firstborn, at his expense. He began to feel a little jealous, and this added to the shadows that were beginning to loom. Then James was seriously ill and nearly died. His prolonged visits to the hospital added further to the worries that affected my mother, even more than my father, and so a further dimension to their dilemma developed.

"By the time I was born, my father said, he had entered into what he could only describe as an emotional limbo-land where the feelings, the emotions, the passions that had once been so important in their relationship seemed to have all but disappeared. My mother seemed to find herself in a similar plight.

"It was then that Gus turned up. He'd apparently been an old flame of my mother's before my father had reappeared on the scene. My mother always denied it, but that was my father's story anyway! The fact was that he'd certainly been very friendly with my mother before he left home to become a Benedictine at Belmont Abbey in Hereford, where he later became abbot. Despite my father's suspicions, he immediately took to the young monk, who had an easy and genial manner that endeared him to all who met him. He was on extended home leave because his mother was ill, and he was busy working on the translation of a book on mystical theology by Anselm Stolz, a German Benedictine, that was eventually published in 1938 under the English title of *The Doctrine of Spiritual Perfection.*

"His name was Aiden Williams in religion, though my mother always called him Gus. He was a deeply spiritual man and although he claimed to have no expertise as a marriage counselor, he was able to show my parents that their love had not come to an end but to a new beginning. Love, he taught them, can never be judged in this life by feeling, but by giving, by giving even when you don't feel. In fact the most perfect expression of love in this life has been made manifested in a quality of loving that goes on giving while asking nothing in return. This is the highest form of loving possible on earth. This is the meaning of the Cross — it is a symbol not just for Christians but for all men and women who want to enter into the fullness of life. Only through a spiritual dying to self through selfless giving can a person open themselves fully to the love without which life has no ultimate meaning.

"He showed them how, with the best will in the world, the most idealistic of men and women will always come to an impasse in their spiritual journey, when the poverty of their own imperfect love suddenly becomes a barrier to receiving, in ever greater measure, the love they want to receive without measure.

"At this point the celibate or the married lover has to undergo a profound purification within, so that the self-centered lover, who is always lurking just below the surface in the adolescent lover, can be taught how to grow up, by learning to love like an adult — in other words, by learning to give time and time again, especially when they receive nothing in return. This is how an adolescent becomes an adult, when, once purified at least in some measure, the journey they have already embarked upon can be resumed on a higher level.

"He convinced my parents that they were both on the verge of an exciting new development in their married life — if they could only forget about themselves and grow up into adult lovers by continually recommitting themselves to one another, no matter what they felt. With his encouragement and advice, they made a new start in the journey they were both beginning to feel had come to an end.

"As they came through that first major crisis in their married love, my father discovered, in the months and years that followed, how a new dimension gradually began to open out in their life together. Precisely because they had suffered and sacrificed together as they mutually supported one another in transcending the adolescent love that seeks only exciting and exhilarating experiences as the sign of its success, they became surer and securer in each other's love. If their love could remain unmoved by the terrible shake-up they had both had to experience, then it must be strong, stronger than before it was tested.

"A new and more perfect experience of love now began to develop in their relationship, that my father could only characterize by the words 'height' and 'depth.' There were moments when they were bonded together more perfectly than ever before, when they were united in mind, heart and body in an experience that bordered on the ecstatic, an experience that is completely unknown to the person whose idea of love never rises above the purely physical.

"Gus explained to them that these moments were to be especially prized, precisely because they signified the moment when the sacrament in which they had committed themselves to one another reached its climax. In the sacrament of marriage, the couple themselves are the ministers — not just on their wedding day, but on every day when they give themselves to one another in pure, selfless love.

"The most sacred moment of that sacrament is when the couple are bonded together to one another, in every way possible here on earth. Then they give to each other their hearts, their minds and their bodies as a means of giving their inner selves, through a union that will grow deeper and deeper, and bond them ever more fully to each other in their mutual journey into the perfect love that will have no end this side of eternity.

"He taught them how to savor these moments, as one should savor the bodily union with Christ in the Sacred Mystery. He taught them how, when they had mutually reached the climax of their loving, they should remain still, side by side, to assimilate and digest what they had both given and both received, or even physically leave each other for a time so that not even each other's presence could distract them from the Presence of the One whom they had just ministered to the other. He even tempered my mother's enthusiasm for early rising to go to the sacrament in the church, when the sacrament of their marriage could be celebrated in her own home with the minister she had been leaving behind. You can minister Christ to each other where you are, he told them, by exercising the sacrament to which you have both committed yourselves.

"What was received in these sacred moments led them both into a deep spiritual peace, not only immediately after these sacred celebrations, but through the rest of their day, as the profound peace that they experienced began to seep out to irrigate the rest of their lives. This is what my father meant by using the word 'depth.' This new understanding of their married love did not mean that all their troubles were over, all their problems behind them — far from it! What it did mean was that because of this new development all the troubles, all the problems which they did have to face, could be faced, because they could be faced together, with an inner strength from God that they had ministered to each other.

"They didn't have an easy ride through the rest of their married life. Remember that we are talking about the thirties. My father, by force of circumstance had to go into the family business. They had a number of shops just south of Manchester, but nobody was interested in buying furniture in the depression. They were hard times for everybody, and what money people did have wasn't spent on refurbishing their homes, but their stomachs.

"Then there were family troubles to be faced, not least the trouble I gave them with this." Peter struck his heavily built-up boot with his stick and then tapped the iron caliper that supported it. "I got polio in the late 1930's shortly after David, my youngest brother, was born. I gave them more than enough trouble, I can tell you. Then, just as there were signs that business was beginning to pick up, the war broke out in 1939. It was like being dropped back into the depression, that is if you depended on selling furniture for your living. My dad worked in an armaments factory during the war years, earning virtually nothing to be added to the nothing that was coming in from his shops. Yes, they were difficult times!

"The war had hardly ended when my mother's father died, then her sister and finally her mother in 1950. They all had long, lingering illnesses that took their toll especially on my mother. Then my eldest brother, James, fell down the Metro steps in Paris and was killed instantly. I'm not trying to bore you with our family's troubles, but just to show you how the love my parents had learned and continued to learn grew with the years, not in spite of but because of the sacrifices they both had to make. It grew and blossomed into a love that continued to sustain them through so many difficult times that they had to face together.

"A dramatic change took place in the late fifties. All of a sudden my older brother, Tony, left home to become a priest. I left home for good to make my home in the Outer Hebrides. Then I retired to my present hermitage on the island of Calvay at the

23

same time that David went to the novitiate to become a Franciscan priest like Tony.

"All of a sudden, my parents found themselves alone after over twenty-five years of married life. Now a second crisis had to be faced, and my father said that for him it was far worse than the first. Here he was, alone with my mother, in the house that had once been so full of noise and activity that had kept his mind well away from the thoughts that now began to rise to tantalize and taunt him. He was middle-aged now, and as he began to look back on his life it seemed to him to be marked by a singular lack of achievement. He hadn't wanted to become a glorified furniture salesman. He had wanted to go to university. He had all the qualifications, he had even been accepted, when his father suddenly dropped down dead at the age of forty-seven. My father had no choice. He had a mother to support, and two younger sisters. Duty came before everything else. All the idealism that he'd had in his youth, all the great ideas, the ambitions that had once inspired him, seemed to have come to nothing. It was too late now to do anything about them.

"Then he began to look forward, and what did the future hold for him save a steady downhill journey to the grave? He began to go through the middle-age crisis that he'd hardly thought of before. He became depressed. He became angry, and his anger and his frustrations began to show — began to affect not only him but the one who meant most to him in the world. My mother was going through a similar crisis which was exacerbated by the menopause that started in her late forties. My father admitted that he became so absorbed in himself and in his own problems that he couldn't see beyond them, not even to the God who'd sustained him in the past but whose very existence he began to doubt in the present. Thank God they had the humility to realize that they needed help. So they took a plane to Rome, ostensibly on pilgrimage, but in fact it was to see Gus. His time as abbot had come to an end, and he had been posted to Sant' Anselmo as the Procurator General of his Order.

"Once again they received the understanding, the encouragement and the help that they needed. 'The last time the crisis was about feeling, wasn't it?' he said to my father. 'This time it's a lot deeper. It's about pride, isn't it? Now you're having to face truths about yourself that you've never had to face before, and it hurts the pride of a man who once thought the world was his to be changed. There are usually two major crisis points in adult love. The first is about feelings and the second is about pride. The first is sensual, the second is spiritual. A great mystical writer called Saint John of the Cross,' he told them, 'called the first of these crisis points the "Dark Night of the Senses," and the second he called the "Dark Night of the Spirit." He may well have been writing particularly for religious in his own way of life, but what he says applies to people of every way of life who are prepared to push on beyond the frontiers of adolescent love to have their love purified and refined in adult love. This love can only be learned by those who are prepared to go on giving without counting the cost, whether they feel like it or whether they don't, no matter how frustrated they may become by the experience of their own inadequacy that will ultimately be laid bare.'

"He took my father to task and told him that the source of his wounded pride that was at the root of his mid-life depression was that he'd forgotten the Christian ideals that he'd been trying to live by, and suddenly reverted to paganism, at least in theory. He had looked round in envy at his contemporaries who'd become professional whizz kids and risen to positions of power and pre-eminence. He had looked at the entrepreneurs who'd taken the business world by storm and ended up millionaires, at the social and political climbers who'd caught the public eye and convinced themselves that they were the leaders of the latest cultural, artistic and intellectual fashions. My father remembered him saying, 'No man who puts his shoulder to the plough and looks back is fit for the Kingdom of Heaven.' He remembered being told in no uncertain terms to stop looking round, to stop looking back, but to look only forward at the furrow he had decided to follow from the first.

"Gus told him that the way they'd been living out their married life had been an inspiration to him and to many others who'd been so impressed by the way they'd lived and loved one another, by the way they'd brought up such a fine family. He explained to them a theological theory close to his own heart, more common in the Eastern Church than in the West — the theory of physical redemption that had been developed particularly by the Greek Fathers, the short of which is that redemption, salvation, is brought about by touch, the touch of God. Christ is the touch of God, whose physical Presence sanctified a world of matter and form, of flesh and blood, by entering into it. Then through touch He communicated the love that filled Him to others, who would go out and by their physical presence, their touch, would communicate what they had received to others.

"This, he explained, was the meaning of the laying on of hands that has characterized the sacraments from the beginning. Love is communicated by touch. This is the tradition that literally hands on the faith that isn't firstly a body of facts but a Body full of love, raised up on the first Easter Day to enter into all who would receive the touch of life. The Apostles, already touched by the holy Presence, were penetrated through and through by it on the first Pentecost day and went out to communicate what they had received to others. The hands, then, that touch and transmit the life of God to you at baptism were themselves the recipients of a touch that can be traced without break all the way back to Jesus.

"Gus explained to them how the physical and intimate loving that was at the heart of their married life was a profound continuation of this process, and not just a continuation but a celebration, in which the love they both received in the sacred touch of baptism was progressively brought to perfection. Not only did their physical marital loving bring Christ's life to birth again in each of them, but it overflowed on to the children who'd been the fruit of their loving. Far from despairing at having produced nothing, they should rejoice in the love that they had mutually generated, a love that was now literally embodied in their sons, who'd in their turn communicated to others what they had received from the touch of their parents.

"My father couldn't speak highly enough of all that Gus had done for them and what his brotherly support did to enable them to begin again, to make a fresh start. Once again they recommitted themselves to each other, not once but many times over, as they gradually emerged from their mid-life crisis closer to one another than they'd ever been before. Once again they received the strength from one another to face all the trials and tribulations that assailed them as they journeyed on into old age. There were joys, too, like the joys of being present at their sons' professions, seeing two of their sons ordained. But there were sorrows that tested their faith to the limits, like the agony they went through when my brother Tony told them he was leaving the priesthood and the religious life and was going to get married. I went with them to South Africa to talk things through with him and help him to do the right thing. With hindsight, I can say that he did do the right thing, make the right decision, but it did not seem so at the time, and it took my parents many years to come to terms with what he did.

"Then they'd hardly got over that when they had a phone call from Barra to say that I was lost at sea, presumed dead. They were devastated and their grief was all the more difficult to bear because no body had been found. They came back from the memorial service almost inconsolable. The tragedy was, when I did suddenly reappear, the shock was so great that my mother had a minor heart attack that was in some ways the beginning of the end for her, although it was years before she died.

"My father said that it was in the last two years that he came to realize just how close they had become. He said that they'd never been more profoundly in love than they had been during my mother's last illness. Gone were the powerful passions and the strong sexual desires that were so important in the earlier days. They'd been important, they'd done their job, they'd played their part in leading them onwards toward a love that was brought as near to perfection as is possible this side of the grave.

"And now my poor dad's all alone, all alone and utterly desolate, beyond all consolation. Whatever will become of him?"

Peter was talking as if in a trance. He buried his face in his hands and remained motionless for several minutes. When he took his hands away I could see two tell-tale tears running down his cheeks.

"I'm sorry," he said, "it's all been too much for me, these last few days. It's not so much my mum I'm thinking about, it's my poor dad. Whatever will he do without her? Whatever will he do without her?"

I didn't know what to say, so I said nothing.

After a minute or two more of silence, Peter raised his eyes from the floor and turned to me, sighed, tried to force a smile and said, "Do you know, I woke up this morning thinking of the film *Wuthering Heights*. I could see it all so clearly — the final scene, I mean, when Heathcliffe finally died and was buried beside his beloved Catherine. The film ended with the wraiths of each rising from the graves like two mysterious mirages made of mist. They merged into each other and went out on to their beloved moor. It's a picture that keeps coming back into my mind — it's a symbol of what it will be like one day when their love will finally be complete.

"Meantime, my mother's love must be brought to further perfection in a purgatory beyond the grave, while my father's purgatory will be here on earth. I don't know who will suffer more, but I do know it will have an end and that end will be a new beginning, for the continuation of their journey together when no barrier of any sort can separate them from the love that will never end, not this side of the eternal hills.

"I'm sorry," said Peter, getting up. "I've overindulged myself. I began by trying to answer your problems and I've ended up by loading you with mine. Come, let's have a cup of coffee and then we'll get down to business — your business this time, not mine!"

3

Peter hadn't overin- dulged himself, at least as far as I was concerned. He had spoken so movingly about his parents that I was almost moved to tears myself on several occasions.

"Do you know," said Peter as he placed a cup of coffee in front of me, "I believe the greatest gift I've ever been given is the love my parents had for one another. The love they worked for over the years overflowed on to all of us. Without that love, I'd be nothing."

Peter drew up a chair and sat opposite me at the kitchen table.

"Thank you for sharing such a personal story with me," I said. "I feel privileged."

"Not at all. To be honest, I think I needed to speak to someone. I didn't do it for that reason, but it's helped me a lot."

"It's helped me, too," I said, "to appreciate something that I've never realized before. It's so easy for priests and religious to patronize lay people, particularly married people, as if they're second-class travelers on the journey upon which we think we are the only guides. They often know much more about the journey than we do, at least in the only way that really matters."

"You're so right," said Peter. "My mother and father knew experientially all about the mystic way. They'd been through their dark nights all right, though I'm sure they'd never heard of Saint John of the Cross, and they'd laugh if you'd told them they were mystics. And yet, I've told you about their journey to help you on yours."

"It has helped me already, Peter, I can assure you. I can only thank you again for describing their journey in such detail."

"Oh, I didn't tell you all the details," said Peter, smiling as if to himself. "That would have taken far too long and I think it would have been too harrowing, too."

Peter stared at the table in front of him. I looked out of the window at nothing in particular. I knew Peter was near to tears. He told me that his father had had a very vivid dream the night before in which he saw Peter's mother as a little girl again, handing him a love-letter under the school desk.

"It's strange," he said. "Even at that age there was something between them that was very special."

"That's what you called juvenile love," I said, hastily interrupting Peter, trying to raise the emotional tone of the conversation to a more intellectual key, for my own sake if not for his!

"Yes, that's right," said Peter, sitting up and pulling himself together. "The point that I was trying to make was that when we first pray, the words we use have been learned from others, from our parents, teachers or perhaps from a prayer book. The language may be full of meaning, full of feeling, taken from the Scriptures or composed by the saints, but it rarely corresponds to the feelings of a beginner.

"That's what I meant by Juvenile Prayer. Perhaps it's pushing things a bit too far, but it just seemed to me that the similarity merited paralleling the two."

"In no way," I said. "I think it's a good analogy and it's worth making, but the prayer of a beginner is also characterized by a lot of asking too. Isn't it? I know it was in my case! I used to think God was a sort of spiritual Father Christmas who would give me whatever I needed, or whatever I thought I needed."

"You're right," said Peter, "but once again there's no real feeling for God. He is just used for what we can get out of Him. Adolescent Prayer starts when the beginners are in some way touched by the presence of God that makes them want to be touched again and again."

"What do you mean by being touched by God? That's never happened to me!"

"Oh yes it has," said Peter. "Why did you come to me in the first place?"

"I'd almost forgotten about that," I said. "But it wasn't because of some strange touch of God, it was because of a young mother I met at a retreat center in London, who gave me your address."

"That's right," said Peter, "but why did you go to that retreat center in the first place? Remember, you went because you came to realize that your prayer life was in a mess! And what made you realize that? It was a touch of God, wasn't it?

"Let me explain how these touches come about in the first place, so that a beginner is inspired to take the next step in their spiritual journey. Let me give you a few examples to show you what I mean. You may be at a party, having a good time with your friends. There's plenty of fun and games, plenty of food and drink. There's music and dancing and everything is in full swing when suddenly it happens."

"What happens?" I said.

"A touch of God," said Peter. "It's not a physical, it's a spiritual touch, that amidst all the merriment makes you suddenly feel alone. It makes you feel that you don't belong, makes you want something further, something higher, something nobler, though you'd be hard put to give a name to what you really do want if someone pressed you. But if you were pressed you'd probably say 'God,' not Jesus Christ but just God.

"On the other hand, you might be sitting by the sea, listening to the waves lap against the shingle on the shore; the sun bloods the sea red as it settles down to rest behind the distant hills. There's a gentle caressing breeze, the sound of the curlew piping over the marshes — then it happens again! A touch.

"When this happens you can close your eyes. You have no

need to gaze at the scene any longer to savor the One who has reached out and touched you through what you have seen. You are enveloped by deep melancholic sadness that is worth all the joys of the world ten times over.

"When I was in Paris I was taken to see the opera *Aida*. It simply bowled me over. The music wasn't entirely new to me but the overall effect of the production was beyond all my expectations. When the curtains fell at the end of the Grand March I was literally entranced. I didn't want to go to the bar with the others for a discussion on the merits or demerits of the current production. I just wanted to be transported back into the solitude of my own room to savor what I had received. Somehow, through the medium of the composer's music, I had been able to experience something of the beauty, something of the glory and majesty of God, and I didn't want the experience to be dissipated by a lot of meaningless claptrap. A moving film, a beautiful piece of music or an artistic masterpiece can have the same sort of effect. Intense study can lead to a similar experience."

"Yes, I'm with you," I said. "I know exactly what you mean. But why should God suddenly decide to reach out and touch us in this way?"

"Well, it's not quite like that," said Peter. "Remember, Saint John said that God is love. I think it would be more accurate to say that God is loving, and He is loving all the time. The reason why we don't experience His loving is because we are so lost in ourselves. Then, all of a sudden, by the combination of some powerful external stimulus and an inner receptivity of mind and heart, we are able to experience for a short time the love of God that is there all the time.

"I used to call these experiences 'mystical premonitions' because that's really what they are. They are an experience in advance of the mystical awareness of God that eventually becomes far more commonplace for the true contemplative who has been sensitized to God's presence through a long purification. These touches actuate a sort of holy restlessness that enables a person to know by experience what Saint Augustine meant when he said, 'Our hearts are restless until they rest in You.' Now they want to search for the One who has touched them, to experience in ever fuller measure the love without measure that has briefly reached out to them."

"And this, I suppose, is what's meant by a call from God, a call to the religious life," I said.

"Good gracious, no!" said Peter, laughing. "You religious are incorrigible! It's not a special call to the religious life, but to the fullness of life that's for all.

"Long before my father met my mother again when he was in his late teens, he knew all about the experiences that we've been talking about. The geography master at school had interested him in astronomy and he used to stay up to all hours on the school roof gazing at the stars. To start with, his knowledge was purely academic; to end with, it was purely mystical. He didn't bother with the telescope when the grandeur and majesty of the heavens spoke to him and touched him with the sort of knowledge that you don't find in books.

"The same thing happened with mountaineering. He started to climb the highest peaks he could find, because, as Mallory said, they were there, but he ended up climbing them because he experienced that Someone else was there. His mother told him he'd fallen in love with love when she saw him daydreaming and she was right, he had. But he didn't see his experiences as a call to religious life, and it never crossed his mind for a moment that he should be a priest or a religious. But he did want to know more fully and experience more deeply the One whose Presence had touched him in those mysterious moments that made him mourn for his Maker.

"That Presence reached out to him in a new and unexpected way the day he re-met my mother. She was to be for him an even greater and more perfect embodiment of the One he was searching for.

"When my father met my mother again, he came to

experience through her something of the beauty, the goodness and the truth of God clothed in a feminine form that excited his heart, his mind and his body and led him on into an experience in which God's Presence made itself felt more fully than ever before. It was an experience that became more and more perfect as, with the passing years, the selfishness that still kept them apart was gradually purified through the suffering and self-sacrifice involved in bringing up a family together."

"I'd never looked at things like that before," I said. "I'd certainly never seen marriage as a call to the mystical life."

"I know you hadn't," said Peter, laughing to himself. "Few religious do. Please do be clear about this — everyone is called to the mystical life, because the mystical life is the expression used by Christian tradition to describe the experience of being plunged ever more fully into the love of God. This is for all, whether they are married, unmarried or celibate.

"I have been stressing the idea in the married life because my own parents came as close as any I have ever known to attaining it, and secondly because that ideal has a lot we celibates can learn from. I don't want to pretend that the ideal is attained more regularly in married life than it is in religious life, because I don't believe it is. I think honors would be about even. You probably had experiences yourself similar to my father, but you interpreted them as a call to religious life."

"Yes, that's right," I said. "And I was also inspired by some religious I met who embodied the ideal I wished to attain. But I suppose if you think about it, the One who reached out to me from them was the One who reached out and touched me in those other special moments that we've been speaking about."

"Precisely," said Peter.

"Are we talking about something that is a particularly Christian experience, or does everyone experience God's touch?"

"It's for everyone," Peter replied emphatically. "God loves everyone, not just Christians, but Christians do respond in a unique way."

"How do you mean?"

"Could I borrow your breviary for a moment?"

"Sure."

"Thanks. Let me see now," said Peter, as he opened it at the readings that had been set for the feast of Saint Augustine.

"Now just listen to this. Here is a classic example of what we've been talking about, what I've described as a mystical premonition or touch. Augustine's reaction to it is typical and his response is specifically Christian as we'll see, though it's interesting to remember he wasn't actually a Christian at the time."

"'When first I knew You, You lifted me up so that I might see that there was something to see, but that I was not yet the man to see it. And You beat back the weakness of my gaze, blazing upon me too strongly, and I was shaken with love and with dread. You called and cried to me and broke open my deafness and You sent forth Your beams and shone upon me and chased away my blindness. You breathed fragrance upon me, and I drew in my breath, and do now pant for You. I tasted You, and now hunger and thirst for You. You touched me, and I have burned for Your peace. So I set about finding a way to gain the strength that was necessary for enjoying You. And I could not find it until I embraced the mediator between God and man, the man Christ Jesus, who is over all things, who was calling unto me and saying, I am the way, the truth, and the life.'

"You see," said Peter, "the experience Augustine had was one that is in many ways common to many, though few can explain the experience as he can. Many people have what are sometimes called natural mystical experiences, but while they spend their lives talking about these precious moments, trying to transpose them into words, capture them in sublime poetry, Augustine rushes on to seek the source from which they came.

"His search leads him to Jesus Christ, for he finds in Him the Masterpiece of God's creation. The fragments of God's beauty and goodness and truth that are scattered in the rest of creation are to be found fully in the Masterwork. He spent years getting to know

Jesus by poring over His every word in the Scriptures and by responding in his own words until a sort of spiritual conversation developed in his prayer life. To begin with, the knowledge was predominantly intellectual, but it gradually became more and more emotional as he experienced the love of Christ reaching out to envelop his mind and heart and his whole being. Now he began to respond in the language of love as his deepest feelings awoke to the love he experienced reaching out to envelop him. Finally, when everything had been said that needed to be said, he found that all he wanted to do was to be still to savor in silence what he had received in a deep but 'heart-felt' contemplative stillness. This was Saint Augustine's spiritual adolescence and it followed an identical pattern to that of my own parents when they rediscovered each other as teenagers.

"When they met again my father had to get to know my mother all over again, but in a deeper way than before when they were only children. Their relationship grew and developed in a way that perfectly parallels the adolescent prayer life of Saint Augustine. When they first began to see each other again they spent hours talking, catching up on the lost years, talking about the present and sharing their plans for the future. They found they had so much in common, they both liked the same sort of music and began to go to concerts together regularly.

"They liked swimming, too, and went to the local pool every Friday evening. My father was delighted to hear that my mother was a keen walker, and they would go hiking in the Peak District on weekends and to the Lake District in the holidays, and of course they loved gazing at the stars together, though the poor stars were regularly neglected! He said they talked a lot to begin with, but the more they met the less they said, the more the spark of love that was there from the beginning began to flicker into a flame, the less they needed words to communicate how they felt, though words were still important.

"On one occasion, he said, they spent almost a whole day on the hills above Lake Windermere and they hardly spoke a word.

He could hardly hold his tears back as he quoted from one of his favorite poems by John Donne, 'The Extasy':

> We like sepulchral statues lay;
> All day, the same our postures were,
> And we said nothing, all the day.

"The same sort of idea is expressed by D.H. Lawrence in *Women in Love*. 'Words travel between the separate parts but in the perfect one there is a perfect silence of bliss.'"

Peter paused for a few moments for his words to sink in before he continued.

"Saint Augustine knew it was Christ whose love he experienced enveloping his whole being as his spiritual adolescence reached its climax, but my parents didn't. That is until Abbot Williams explained who they experienced in the love that they mutually generated and shared. It was a sacramental love because each was a seeable, touchable sign to the other of the different quality of God's love that they shared with each other. This sacramental love was publicly celebrated on their wedding day, and on every other day throughout their lives whenever they tried to love each other selflessly."

"Thank you, Peter," I said, "for explaining everything to me so clearly. It does make sense to me, although when you were describing how Saint Augustine's prayer life reached its climax I thought he'd reached the heights of mystical prayer."

"Oh no!" said Peter. "Only the heights of Adolescent Prayer."

"Well, what happened next?" I asked.

Peter laughed. "You should know," he said, "you've just been finding out for yourself when your spiritual adolescence suddenly came to an end."

"You mean Saint Augustine had to go through what I've been going through?" I asked.

"Exactly!" said Peter. "And so does everyone else when spiritual adolescence suddenly comes to an end as it did for you."

"But why does this have to happen?" I said.

"It has to happen," said Peter, "so that a person can grow up spiritually and enter into what I've called Adult Prayer, where they are prepared for Perfect Prayer. You see, the reason these fleeting experiences of God that we spoke about before could not continue for long was because the would-be mystic belongs to this world, not the next, and so does his heart. And his heart is full of so many human desires of one sort or another that are initially far stronger than the transitory desire for God.

"If purely human desires are allowed to absorb the whole of a person's attention, then these brief mystical glimpses of God will diminish the older a person gets until they will play little or no part in their experience. You see this sort of thing happening in the lives of some of the major and many of the minor romantic poets. The more human needs and desires absorb their attention, then the less they can be sensitive and attentive to the source of their inspiration in creation. Their poetry suffers and so do they. Time and time again they turn to sex, to drink, to drugs, to do for them what the touch of God had done before, or at least to satisfy the yearnings that that touch had uncovered within them.

"Those Christians who, like Augustine, turn to prayer to lead them on to come to know and experience the Creator in His Masterwork, travel on a path that is unknown to most of the poets. They begin to experience the touch of God reaching out to them not just from inanimate creation but from a living Person. Through prayer, they are not only touched in the highest part of their spiritual being but in every part of their being, as their human emotions are opened up and begin to respond to the One who excites the sensual as well as the spiritual.

"Although their love is expressed in words, words finally fail them and all they want to do is to gaze in awe at the One who absorbs their whole attention. This 'mystical gaze' is not totally different from that of the natural mystic, but it is surrounded and supported by a wealth of human feelings and emotion. Medieval spiritual writers used the words *meditatio, oratio,* and *contemplatio* to describe how an initial intellectual process develops through highly charged emotional aspirations to the still and silent gaze. During the Counter-Reformation, when spiritual writers became a little more analytical and psychological, they used the terms Meditation, Affective Prayer, Prayer of Simplicity, and Acquired Contemplation to describe what their medieval forebears had described before them. The phrase 'acquired contemplation' was coined to describe the final stage of this process because it can be reached by human endeavor, to distinguish it from true mystical contemplation which, as we will see, is a pure gift of God that cannot be attained by any man-made methods or techniques."

"I'm with you," I said. "I know what you're saying from my own spiritual reading, but in my arrogance I had come to believe that when I came to what you've called acquired contemplation I'd reached the heights, and so I was shattered when everything seemed to stop almost overnight. Despite everything I tried to do, I got nowhere but deeper and deeper into a spiritual desert with no oasis in sight."

"You see, what happened was this," said Peter. "The initial fleeting experiences of God's Presence that reached out to touch you actuated a deep desire to be touched again and again. It was this desire that led you to take up a serious prayer life, knowing that it was only there that this desire would be fulfilled. What was initially a rather vague desire for some sort of experience changed into a desire for a person. Just as a teenager who falls in love with love and moons around looking for some sort of experience to satisfy them changes when they discover not just love, but someone's love reaching out to embrace them. The experience of being loved deepens as you come to know the one who loves you. The same thing happens in prayer as the desire for love is changed into a desire for the Lover.

"Given serious commitment to prayer, love grows and grows with the ever deepening knowledge of the Lover that comes through listening to His words and discovering that they are not only charged with meaning that you had not understood before, but loving that you had not experienced before. This is why the slow meditative reading of the words of Jesus in the Sacred Scriptures have always been the primary way that the heart and mind of the believer is raised to the Father through the Son.

"As the desire that was there from the beginning is buoyed up by human feelings and emotions, it is able to remain focused on God and to remain so for longer periods of time than before. Prayer now becomes no more than a simple, silent, contemplative gaze upon God, and words are only used occasionally to redirect its high point. Adolescent Prayer has reached a climax which suddenly changes when the heart's desire, that had been sustained and supported by a whole range of human emotions before, is suddenly raised above and beyond them as it reaches out into the unknown. It's as if it has suddenly fastened on to some mysterious magnetic power that draws it relentlessly towards itself. Once this happens, Adolescent Prayer comes to an abrupt end. There can be no going back even if a person wanted to. The days of this exciting, exhilarating, emotional prayer have ended, never to return in quite the same way again.

"Let me give you an analogy to explain a little more clearly what has happened. When a rocket or spaceship destined for the planet Mars is ready to depart, it has attached to it boosters, huge canisters of fuel whose job it is to raise it up off the ground and out of the earth's atmosphere. When they have done this they will be of no further value, so they must be detached from the spaceship or they would impede its progress towards its destination. As the spaceship comes closer to Mars it comes under the planet's magnetic force and travels faster and faster. The boosters or the canisters of fuel, then, fulfill exactly the same function for the spaceship as do the emotions for the heart's desire for God. They raise it up off the ground, as it were, where it has been earthbound. They raise it higher and higher for as long as it takes to latch on to the mysterious magnetic pull of the divine love that it has been gazing upon through its most perfect human embodiment. When they have done this they can do no more and must be cast away or they would impede their progress towards God."

"I see," I interrupted, "and that's what happened to me."

"Yes," said Peter. "That's why you can't use your emotions in prayer as you could before. That's why all spiritual feeling that sustained your first fervor in the prayer groups and in your private prayer can no longer support you in the journey ahead. You have to learn a new means of prayer that will sustain you on the mystic way that you have now just begun. You have now left Adolescent Prayer for good. Adult Prayer has already begun. My job is to help you on the road ahead."

Peter was on his feet, smiling. He could see that his explanation had had the desired effect. Yes, it did make sense to me. A thousand and one questions were rising up in my mind, but I could see they would have to wait. It was almost one o'clock and I knew Peter had to go.

"When can we meet again?" I said eagerly. I'd been so engrossed in what Peter had been saying that I'd forgotten all about his mother's death and about his father and his own grief.

"Oh, I'm so sorry!" I said. "You've got more than enough on your plate at present."

"No," said Peter, "I invited you here precisely so that we could talk. But I do have to go to Liverpool with my father tomorrow morning. He'd just put down a deposit on a flat fifty yards away from my brother's home. He'd planned spending the rest of his retirement there with my mother so that they could watch the boys grow up. My brothers were both keen on the idea, and if anything happened to one of them the other would be close by so that they could be looked after — but now everything's changed. Tony's insisting that my father should move in with him, so we'll have to try and get out of the contract. Anyway, I'll be back by lunchtime, so I'll come round about two o'clock if that's all right by you."

"Fine," I said.

"Bye," said Peter, and **4** with that he was gone.

It was half-past two before Peter arrived, apologizing for keeping me waiting.

"Sorry," he said, "but the negotiations proved longer and more difficult than we had anticipated. We couldn't get out of the contract — it had been signed and sealed, so my father had to either go ahead or lose his deposit. In the end we thought it more sensible to forgo the money, otherwise my father would have been landed with a flat that he didn't want and it would have cost him more than the deposit to resell it, not to mention all the trouble that he could well do without. Anyway, I've had enough of all that for one day. How are you? Have you had any time to think over the things that we were talking about yesterday?"

"Oh yes," I said, "I'm so grateful for all you said and for explaining everything so clearly, but I have a thousand and one questions that I would like to ask you."

"I thought you might," said Peter, "but if you don't mind I'm not going to let you ask me any of them — at least for the time being. You see, when we started I said I was going to begin by outlining a map of prayer from the beginning to the end of the journey, so that you could see the way ahead with as much clarity as possible. When I've done that then we'll come back to see where you are on that journey with a far clearer idea of the way ahead."

"Yes," I said, "I see what you mean. Your approach makes sense. I'll try and contain myself until you've finished outlining your map of prayer."

"Right," said Peter, "Let me continue. The first point that I want to make is that my parents went through exactly the same experience as you in their married loving, just as other married couples do. Their adolescent loving came to an end when the powerful feelings, emotions and passions that drew them closer and closer to each other finally led them on to experience the divine love reaching out to them through the human. This is precisely why marriage is called a sacrament, because it enables a man to experience something of the divine love reaching out to touch him through the touch of this woman, loving him through the love of this woman, embracing him through the embrace of this woman, and vice versa. The experience of the divine love makes them hunger and thirst for more of what they have received and leads them to something of a crisis in their relationship with each other. The experience of the divine love that they have transmitted to each other is strong enough to draw them away from the powerful emotional love that satisfied them so completely before, yet it is not powerful enough to draw them fully into itself.

"The problem is usually exacerbated because one of the partners is inevitably affected before the other. The second partner, noticing the change in the physical intensity of the first, begins to wonder what has happened and is naturally beset by unwarranted doubts. Many novelists like D.H. Lawrence, whom I mentioned to you before, describe this critical point in human loving, and they try to explore the problems, sometimes fatal, that arise for the couple.

"But none of them, at least in my experience, understand what has happened and why it has happened. Even my mother's Benedictine friend Gus, who helped my own parents at their crisis point, didn't understand fully why it had come about. Few people do, but he did give them the best possible help and encouragement to go on. Without his help their relationship could have been ruptured permanently, as it is for so many others. With this help they learned to go on giving, to go on loving, with or without the emotional props that had supported them before. Eventually a new dawn opened for them both, as my father described to me.

"I now find myself in the same predicament as Gus, and you find yourself in the same predicament as my parents. You both started out in different life-styles on the same search but ended up in the same situation. And that situation is where you are now, and the question you want me to answer is — 'What am I to do, how do I proceed from here?' But before I try to take you forward, let me briefly take you back to where you started, to help explain how your present situation arose in the first place.

"The first brief glimpses of the Creator came through creation — it might have been through a magnificent stretch of countryside, it might have come through gazing upon a single blade of grass, an insect crawling through the undergrowth, or a caterpillar climbing up a rose bush. Now, remember what I said to you before — when your contemplation of creation enabled you to experience the Creator, you found yourself drawn inward. It was as if some soothing sedative stilled your mind and heart and made you mourn for your Maker, as for a lost friend or friendship. And yet this strange melancholy was as sweet as it was sad and you wanted it to go on and on and envelop you more and more completely. Once this had happened, you no longer needed to gaze at the scene before you. You could close your eyes and savor what you had received in your mind and in your heart.

"The physical senses and the feelings and emotions that depend upon them have no part in what is primarily a spiritual experience. When the experience vanishes, as it always will, the heart and mind mourn for what has been lost and the heart desires to receive it once more. The restless heart that yearns for love unlimited is a commonplace experience for the young who have been 'touched.' They remain unsatisfied until, in adolescent love, their heart is ravished by powerful human feelings and emotions that raise it up and give it a temporary sense of fulfillment and completion. But when, once again, the heart begins to sense the divine reaching out to touch it, this time through human loving, it desires to experience even more intensely what it had experienced before. Once again the physical senses can sense nothing, they cannot experience the One who is beginning to draw the heart onward, and so they simply fall away, just like the boosters on the spaceship as the magnetic pull of the planet draws it mysteriously towards itself.

"Compared with the powerful emotions and passions aroused in adolescent love, the return of the mysterious Presence seems so subtle, so delicate and so illusory. So much so that, to begin with, a person like yourself experiences little more than an inexplicable restlessness that can't rest in God and doesn't seem inclined to rest in anything else with any satisfaction. There can be no going back. The feelings and the emotions of first fervor will never again return to support you in the same way. The time for meditation is over. Now you must learn to draw all your spiritual resources together and concentrate them on the mysterious love that has already touched your heart, so that it can touch your heart again and again until it possesses it. Then what is received first in your heart will overflow into the rest of your human being.

"In my parents' case, they put their faith in Gus, put aside their doubts and continued to go on giving, go on loving, even when they felt it was pointless, getting them nowhere, and even when it seemed they received nothing in return. Later they realized that that was the time when the quality of their loving was proved again and again, for anyone can love when they seem to receive in return, but only a perfect lover can go on giving when they receive nothing in return. Or rather, a person only *becomes* a perfect lover by giving again and again when they receive nothing in return. It was only because of the quality of their mutual loving that a new dawn did eventually rise in their married love. Then they began to experience a quality of loving that they had never experienced before. There were times when it reached shattering degrees of intensity. Times too when it seemed to spill over into their daily lives, whether they were together or not. You may remember, my father characterized these moments by the words 'height' and 'depth.'

"Now, the same will happen to you if you go forward as they did. I will detail precisely what you must do later, but to continue and complete the overall picture, let me go on. Let's assume that you do go on giving yourself to God in prayer, as faithfully and as consistently as you did when you experienced powerful feelings and emotions supporting you. To begin with, your prayer will be characterized by endless distractions that had been mainly swept aside at the height of first fervor. They will ravage your restless heart, drawing its attention away from the Presence it yearns for, that seems to be enveloped, as it were, in a 'cloud of unknowing.' Then, when you least expect it, the experience of the Presence returns.

"It is initially almost exactly the same as the experience you had before your spiritual adolescence began, but it doesn't seem to be triggered off by any form of external stimulus that is visible to the senses. It arises from within, and it seems to come and go quite irrespective of anything you do, apart, that is, from patiently waiting in an otherwise drab and dreary prayer life, that seems to be full of nothing but a thousand and one distractions that pick and paw at your mind from the inside.

"When the experience of Presence returns the distractions do not totally disappear, but they are not as noticeable as before, as something or Someone begins to absorb your attention. In time and with perseverance and with other suggestions that I will detail later, this subtle experience becomes more and more regular and more deeply engrossing. It is exactly the same experience that preoccupied the poets and the natural mystics, except that it now becomes a far more regular and dependable experience for the person who consistently creates the right inner dispositions of mind and heart to receive it. It is not as capricious as it was before, and it comes and goes quite independently of the outer senses that are now of no more help, and can only hinder the prayer that they could have helped before.

"It's not difficult to explain what comes next, once you understand the nature of the natural mystical experience that drew you into contemplation before first fervor. The same experience just becomes more and more engrossing, more and more absorbing, so that you find yourself drawn into a deep recollectedness that is not of your own making. Then, at a moment when you least expect it, the experience becomes more and more intense and you are raised to a far higher degree of awareness than ever before. Not even the most dramatic and awe-inspiring stretch of countryside or the most exciting and exhilarating musical experience had this effect in the past. The deep, deep absorption of the mind and the heart in this new consciousness is often preceded by a lifting sensation in the inner being, and a gentle sliding back into the recollectedness that preceded it when the experience has peaked and run its course.

"On other occasions, even this experience pales into insignificance as another touch of God raises the heart and mind with such sudden power and force that you don't know what has hit you. Once again the lifting sensation that you had before raises your consciousness higher and higher. You not only feel yourself being raised up with tremendous force, but you feel yourself spiraling, spinning upwards to rest at such a high degree of consciousness that you know you can go no further. At least you know you can go no further while retaining consciousness. Your best hopes, or perhaps your worst fears, are eventually realized when the speed and the power with which you spiral upwards quadruples and ends, not in the highest possible degree of human consciousness, but in complete oblivion, for a greater or lesser period of time that is in no way determined by you."

If the experiences that Peter was talking about were utterly absorbing, and all-engrossing, then so was the explanation of them. I was absolutely fascinated, not just by what he was saying but by the way he was saying it. Although the language was in itself understandably dramatic — how else could he explain himself? — he himself was so calm, as composed as if he were describing experiences that were to him ordinary and commonplace.

All right, I admit I had read my quota of mystical tomes —

I'd read about high mystical experiences, of ecstasies and other phenomena that I didn't understand — but nothing had really made sense to me before. There was no definable logic that enabled me to make sense of anything. It just didn't all hang together. There was at least an order and logic to what Peter was saying, even though the experiences he detailed were quite beyond my experience — yet I had experienced that subtle recollectedness, both before and after the first fervor that now seemed to me something of a waste of time.

"Now," said Peter, preparing to continue, "various names have been given to these experiences. Some writers, like Saint John of the Cross, refer to them in general as touches of God, which is what they are, without distinguishing them from each other, because he's more interested in defining something else that we will have to talk about later. However, the most commonly-known terminology comes from Saint Teresa of Avila from her masterwork, *The Interior Castle,* written when she herself had scaled the heights of mystical prayer.

"The phrase 'Prayer of Recollection' is used by her to describe the first subtle awareness of the presence of God. The subsequent stages of mystical awareness are not categorized, not because they are essentially different experiences from the first, but because they are of greater intensity and therefore capable of absorbing the inner mind and heart more and more fully. Let me explain what I mean. In the Prayer of Recollection the experience is initially so subtle that it is hardly noticeable, and so it does little to dismiss the distractions that swarm around in the mind like a hive of bees. Even when the recollectedness does deepen, the distractions, though partially stilled, are never absent.

"But when the touch of God raises the consciousness higher, the absorption is deeper than ever before. The lifting sensation that usually but not always precedes it draws a person into what she calls the 'Prayer of Quiet.' For the first time, the intensity of the experience is so great that the heart or the will is totally absorbed in the divine touch. It is no longer unduly bothered by the distractions that always pestered it before in the Prayer of Recollection. They are still there, but they are no longer a problem.

"In the Prayer of Recollection, a person's consciousness is rather like a single-story building that is never free of distractions. In the Prayer of Quiet, it's more like a two-story building. On the first floor the heart or the will is totally absorbed in God while a few distractions still remain on the ground floor, but never so as to disturb the absorption of the heart in the upper story.

"With 'Full Union' the power of God's touch is so strong and so all-absorbing that there can be no distractions at all. As the expression 'Full Union' implies, the inner self is totally united with the all-engrossing Presence within. Saint Teresa uses 'Ecstasy' to explain what happens next, when the power of the Presence becomes too much for a weak human nature to sustain so that temporary oblivion follows.

"Sometimes what is experienced inside prayer is experienced outside prayer, but later rather than sooner. At any rate, at the beginning of mystical prayer the inner sense of recollection is so subtle that it would hardly be noticed. Only later as the intensity rises would it be noticed, and even then it is usually swept aside as the work of the day encroaches, only to return in the evening. Sometimes, however, when God's touch is as intense as in Full Union, it can strike outside prayer like a bolt from the blue when you least expect it. You may be tying your shoelace, putting on the kettle or waiting at the checkout counter in the supermarket. Fortunately it lasts for little more than a second or so and leaves you to carry on what you were doing before. Saint Teresa calls these touches 'darts of love,' for that's what they feel like, at least when you get used to them.

"Unfortunately, and to the embarrassment of the recipients, ecstasy can occur as readily outside prayer as within, so they end up not begging God to give them the grace to receive it, but to take it away! The word 'rapture' is usually used to describe short sudden ecstasies that happen like lightning, with the speed of a bullet spiraling out of a rifle, and with a degree of violence that can be frightening. Saint Teresa tried to warn her sisters in advance so that they wouldn't be too alarmed when it happened."

"Peter," I said, suddenly interrupting him, "I've been fascinated by all that you have been saying to me. You've enabled me to see and understand what I've never fully understood before. But one thing doesn't make sense to me, and it's this. If we already had an experience, albeit brief, of the touch of God at the outset of our spiritual journey, couldn't we have begun the mystic way there and then, instead of having to go through what you've called Adolescent Prayer and the first fervor that now seems to have been something of a pointless digression?"

"Well," said Peter, "in theory yes, but in practice no, at least not for those who claim to be Christians, although some non-Christians reach high degrees of mystical consciousness without passing through the sort of spiritual adolescence that I've been talking about. In the early Christian centuries, many pagan philosophers laid special emphasis on the mystical elements in the works of Plato. Through rigorous asceticism they came to experience similar states of prayer to those described by Saint Teresa. Plotinus, who was the most important of these Neoplatonists, had ecstasies identical to those of the Christian mystics. He had many followers in subsequent centuries, particularly in Europe after the Renaissance, when Christian mysticism was in decline. Many Eastern mystics, particularly in India, have had similar experiences of the God who calls all to experience His love, whether they are Christians or not.

"However, the importance of spiritual adolescence is that it helps direct a person's gaze to the place where the fullness of God's love is to be found here on earth, namely in Jesus Christ. By building a prayer life that is centered upon Him, on studying His every word and action, a person begins to find what they are searching for, as they begin to experience something of the fullness of love that alone will satisfy the hunger and thirst that made them set out in the first place.

"This love reaches out, to touch not only their hearts and

minds but their whole beings, including the physical senses that remained for the most part dormant in their first contemplation of creation. In Adolescent Prayer all the forces of the inner mind, the imagination, the memory, the feelings and the emotions, are mobilized to one end, to support, to strengthen and to sustain the heart's desire that would reach out to savor at its source the Savior who has searched them out like the hound of heaven. Once again they perform for the heart or the will what the boosters do for the spaceship. They help to raise it off the ground, as it were, and direct it towards its destination.

"Although I have described a new mystical awakening that takes place beyond spiritual adolescence and some of the profound and lofty experiences that may lie ahead, the immediate future seems bleak. The lush pastures of first fervor give way to a desert where the presence of God seems remarkable only by its absence. Now the traveler has to travel on, supported not by fervor but by faith, and by faith alone. This is why it is called by many the 'Prayer of Faith.' If the traveler continues to journey on in prayer, it will be because of the support which was received in spiritual adolescence, when strong and vibrant human feelings strengthened a weak will with the determination to travel on, come what may. The memory of the close personal and emotional attachment to Jesus Christ that was formed then will help them support the traveler in the spiritual desert ahead. This is why a Christian mystic has such an advantage over others, and that's why, historically, there have been so many more of them.

"If Saint Teresa helps us to understand and appreciate the importance of spiritual oases in the desert, Saint John of the Cross helps us understand and appreciate the importance of desolation. This is why it is important to read them both to get the best possible picture of the way ahead.

"Saint John doesn't use the symbolism of a desert to expound his mystical theology, but the symbolism of a night — a dark night. In his great work *The Dark Night of the Soul,* he calls the first part of the night 'the Dark Night of the Senses' because the physical senses are plunged into darkness at the outset of the mystic way for the reasons that I mentioned before. The Light that seemed to shine so brightly upon them in spiritual adolescence will shine no more until they are purified of all that prevents that Light from transforming them into what they are destined to become.

"He calls the second part of his night 'the Dark Night of the Spirit' because once again the Light that seemed to enlighten the spiritual senses of the mind so well before will enlighten them no longer, until they too are purified.

"Saint John of the Cross doesn't write about first fervor, he assumes it. His work *The Dark Night of the Soul* begins at the point where first fervor has come to an end and the dark night of the soul is about to begin. If you read the first nine chapters or so, you'll see he lists all the faults and failings of spiritual adolescents that prevent them from reaching the mystic union with the One they yearn for. Do read them, you'll have a laugh as you see yourself, your real self that was hidden beneath all the charismatic fervor that made you think you had arrived at the heights and were therefore the ideal guide for everybody else! It is amazing how the 'Old Man' can hide away beneath the fizz and pop of first fervor believing that he is the 'New Man,' and drive everybody mad with his charismatic enthusiasm that is riddled through and through with pride and arrogance if they could only see it!

"When my parents entered into their night of the senses and all the wonderful feelings and emotions seemed to fade away, they had to face their own faults and failings as never before. Naturally they didn't like it, and they began to blame each other for what they didn't like to see in themselves, trying to highlight the splinter in the other's eye so they wouldn't notice the beam that was in their own. In the end, with the help they sought from prayer and the genuine love they had for one another, they were able to see themselves as they were and they confessed, not just to a priest but to each other, and received the mutual forgiveness that bonded them together more deeply than ever.

"When later, in middle age, they saw more deeply into the

source of all their human weaknesses, they had to see the deep-seated pride and prejudice that had always been at work within them. This was their dark night of the spirit."

"So," I said, "the mystic way is really all about purification, purifying us from all the sin and selfishness that keeps God out."

"Exactly," said Peter. "That's why some mystics have called it purgatory on earth, because that's really what it is. Dante picked up an old theme of the Desert Fathers when he said that there is only one way to heaven and that is through hell — or that part of hell that we call purgatory. I suppose you could argue that a saint is a person who has passed through purgatory this side of the grave, while the rest of us go through it on the other.

"I can understand why people have trouble trying to understand hell, but I've never been able to understand why purgatory presents such a problem. It seems common sense to me. How you explain it is one thing, but the reality is quite another. Opposites can never be one unless whatever separates them from one another is cast away. The utterly selfish cannot be at one with the utterly selfless unless one becomes like the other, the selfish like the selfless. Purgatory is just the traditional word used to describe the pain involved when a selfish person undergoes the personal purification involved in becoming selfless. Sure, the fire and brimstone merchants went over the top, and so did the saintly sadists, who presented purgatory as a heavenly torture-chamber just beyond the grave. Their presentation might leave something to be desired but they were at least right about the pain. The pain involved in the dying of the 'Old Man' that the 'New Man' be formed. I'll deal with this in more detail later. For the moment, let me just make the point that no would-be mystic can reach his destination without passing through purgatory either in this world or in the next.

"Saint John of the Cross and Saint Teresa of Avila are a powerful combination — they were both made Doctors of the Church, because they were totally orthodox and safe guides who detailed, in two unique but complementary ways, the purification or the purgatory on earth that takes place on the mystic way. They show in different ways how God works through presence and absence, through light and darkness, through death and resurrection, to purge away everything that prevents a person from entering into an ever fuller union with Himself.

"Once this purification is completed, the union for which the believer craved from the beginning can take place immediately. The very moment that selfishness has been sufficiently purged away is the moment when the necessary likeness to Christ enables the two to become one. Then, for the first time, the mystic can genuinely say, with Saint Paul, 'I live, no, it is no longer I who live but it is Christ who lives in me.' In the dark night of the soul, the sensual and the spiritual which were separated at the beginning of the purification are reunited as one at the end of it and are simultaneously reunited with the Christ who was completely lost to view in its darkest moments."

"Oh, I see," I said, interrupting Peter again. "I'd got it all wrong. I thought that once you'd passed through first fervor you sort of passed through the humanity of Jesus to the divinity, as it were, and the next stage of the mystic way would lead you in some obscure and mysterious fashion into the Godhead, leaving the humanity of Jesus behind for good."

"No! No!" said Peter. "We are not Buddhists, or Sufis or Platonists for that matter. We are Christians! We believe that the fullness of God's life is to be found and experienced in the full humanity of Jesus Christ. Remember what Jesus said to Philip when he asked to be shown the Father — He said, 'Do you not believe that I am in the Father and the Father is in me?' And later, at that same supper table, He promised that those who loved Him and made their home within Him would be one, not only with Him but with the Father who dwelt within Him. Once the mystic has been purified in the night by the Holy Spirit he is ready for this profound Oneness with the Father in the Son that Jesus promised before His death — what classical spiritual writers called the 'Transforming Union,' or the 'Spiritual Marriage.'"

"Is this similar to what goes on all the time that you called the Prayer of Quiet or Full Union?" I said. "Or is it something quite different?"

"No, it is something quite different," said Peter, "something far more human, because it involves not just the mind, not just the soul, but the whole person, the body and the soul, the sensual and the spiritual, the complete human being. The mystical experiences that preceded the Transforming Union are all part and parcel of the purifying process, as the Holy Spirit works in light and in darkness preparing an imperfect human being for a perfect union, a sort of Mystical Marriage with Christ. When this marriage takes place it is not just a union of souls or of spirits but of one human being with another human being by the power of the Holy Spirit, who bonds the Father to the Son. The Christian mystics who have reached the heights are always characterized by the realization that in Christ they have been caught up, body and soul, into the rapturous vortex of life that endlessly revolves between the Father and the Son to eternity."

"I suppose all of this is a completely incommunicable experience," I said.

"Yes, it is," said Peter. "But once again it is just possible to get a glimpse of what this experience feels like, just as it is possible for the natural mystic to glimpse in a small measure what comes later in fuller measure. Let me explain what I mean. Despite its shortcomings, the prayer of first fervor does involve the whole person, body and soul, spiritual and sensual in a single act of loving. The feelings of loving and being loved are not just experienced in the mind and in the heart but in the body too, where they reverberate through the whole range of human emotions. No matter how imperfect the loving of the 'Old Man' might be, it nevertheless contains feelings and experiences that are fully realized when the 'Old Man' is finally transformed into the 'New Man.' The misplaced desire to go back to the first fervor that recurs in the night is in fact a misinterpreted desire to go forward, to experience fully what was only experienced in part in the past. The spiritual completion that everyone yearns for is not to be found finally in the disembodied mysticism of the night, however fulfilling it might seem at times, but in the full-bodied union that takes place in the Mystical Marriage, when the life of the Three in One seems to open out to admit a fourth."

"So all these mystical experiences that you mentioned earlier are part of the inner purification, what Saint John of the Cross calls 'the dark night of the soul'?" I said, as the penny was beginning to drop. "And once the purification ends, the Spiritual Marriage or the Transforming Union begins immediately!"

"That's right," Peter replied.

"Does it just happen out of the blue without any warning at all?"

"No," said Peter, "like any night, it begins with dusk and is darkest of all at midnight, but as the night draws to a close the blackness brightens as the dawn approaches. It's the same with the dark night of the soul. And as the dawn draws nearer, a person begins to glimpse something of the approaching Mystical Marriage in brief transitory experiences, when the whole person is touched by the love that will soon possess them totally. These premonitions are called betrothals, spiritual betrothals, because they are a brief, transitory foretaste of the marriage to come. It's even possible to get some idea of what they feel like by recalling the natural mystical experiences that I used before to explain the mystical contemplation that becomes more and more intense in the night.

"Sometimes when you see or hear something that is of outstanding beauty, like one of the great violin concertos, for instance, performed by a musician of outstanding genius, the performance can not only draw your heart and mind out of yourself into a profound other-worldly experience, it can literally make the hairs on your neck stand up and send a shiver down your spine. I think you know what I mean. It gives you a tingle and you can break out in goose pimples all over your body. It's so well known that there's a program on the radio called *The Tingle Factor,* when celebrities are invited to choose the music, or even the words from a great play or a famous orator, that gives them this experience. It happens when the experience of the 'other-worldly' is so great that it touches not just the heart and mind but the whole person, and can be experienced shimmering through the whole body. It can happen when we are confronted not just by beauty, but by goodness and truth that is seen embodied in some great person whom we admire or look up to, either in real life or, more usually, as portrayed on the stage or on the screen, when a great act of heroism, courage or goodness is re-enacted before us.

"These experiences begin to happen regularly as the spiritual betrothals announce the arrival of the Mystical Marriage. They are usually triggered off by a word or phrase from the Scriptures, or from the liturgy or from a hymn or some other source that speaks of the God with whom it seemed we had lost contact in the night. Suddenly we are touched not only in the heart and mind but in the feelings and emotions too, as we experience a tingle reverberating through our bodies that seemed dead to every sensual touch in the darkest moments of the night. It's like the first movements of a great spiritual thaw, when the heart, the mind and the body, that had been frozen over in the night, begin to melt at the first touch of sunlight as the long-awaited day begins to dawn. Sometimes words that meant nothing for years suddenly touch the emotions with such an impact that the body shivers with delight and the sensation triggers off an ecstasy.

"These ecstasies or raptures can become almost commonplace in the spiritual betrothals, and can carry on for a time even into the Mystical Marriage, where they eventually die out. They are, in fact, caused by the power of the new life that is trying to enter into the whole person, and are signs of the human weakness that cannot cope with it to begin with. But when the Mystical Marriage is complete, the whole person enjoys the new life that bonds them to Christ, in and out of prayer. Then these rather dramatic and unwelcome experiences tend to fade away."

"I see more clearly than ever that I'd got it all wrong!" I said. "I had the idea that the highest reaches of the mystic way consisted in what you called Quiet and Full Union, and rare experiences of ecstasy or rapture when one was totally lost in God."

"I'm afraid you did have it all wrong," said Peter, "but so have so many others. I blame 'Dennis the Menace.'"

"Who?" I said.

"'Dennis the Menace' I called him. He was a mystical writer who lived at the beginning of the fifth century by all accounts. He is thought to have been a Syrian monk deeply influenced by Neoplatonism. His works wouldn't have had much of an impact had he not hit upon the idea of calling himself Dionysius, and claiming to be Dionysius the Areopagite, an Athenian senator who was the convert and friend of Saint Paul. Although later on in history the 'holy deceit' was discovered and he came to be known as the pseudo-Dionysius, it was too late to prevent the reverence for the person he claimed to be, giving his mystical works an importance quite beyond their worth.

"He had an incredible influence on medieval mystics, on the Rhinelanders and on many others up to the present day. So much so that you have been unwittingly influenced by him through the books you have been reading. The Platonists believed that salvation involved freeing the human spirit from its prison, the body, and seeking its perfection in the divine Spirit, hence their attachment to the mystical experiences that precede the Mystical Marriage, experiences which involve only a spiritual union in which the wicked body has no part. Rare moments of ecstasy that Plotinus experienced represented for them the high point of the mystic way.

"True salvation for Christians involves not freeing the spirit of man from his wicked body, but allowing both his spirit and his body to be penetrated through and through by the Holy Spirit who bonds them together as one, to be united to the Perfect One — spirit to spirit, body to body, flesh to flesh. In the Mystical Marriage we see the first flowering of this inner union on earth. Notice it is a marriage, and marriage is not the end of love but a new beginning of love that will deepen and deepen to eternity, because there is no end to the love of the One who loves without measure.

"Good gracious!" said Peter, looking at his watch. "I'll have to be making a move. My poor dad will be wondering what has happened to me. I do feel so sorry for him. He simply doesn't know what to do with himself now that my mother's gone. I think I told you before that he said that the last two years or so with my mother were the happiest days of his life. I think those years were the closest they both came to their Transforming Union here on earth. So much of the selfishness that had separated them throughout their lives had been purified away. They were so close that it was almost as if the physical bodies that had first bonded them together were the only things that kept them apart.

"I do hope the analogy of my parents' love for each other has helped to throw light on what it has enlightened for me. I don't want to give the impression that they were perfect, or candidates for canonization, but they were both very good people. Their journey into an ever-deepening love not only gave me the best possible start in life that I could hope for, but has been a continual inspiration to continue on the same journey that they took, albeit by a different route."

It was half-past five when Peter left, promising to come again the next day at two. I couldn't believe how time had flown; I'd been so enthralled by all that Peter had been saying that time seemed to have stood still. If he'd given me a unique insight into the mystic way in this life, he'd also given me a genuine experience of eternity in the next!

I took *The Dark Night* **5** *of the Soul* to bed with me! I found it on the top shelf of the presbytery library, covered with dust, next to an ancient commentary on canon law. I found the first part fascinating in the light of all that Peter had been saying, but the more I read the more bored I became. Somewhere in the middle of his night I suddenly fell into mine, and didn't wake up until half-past seven the next morning. Thanks to Saint John of the Cross, I had the best sleep in years. What a shame his works are always languishing beneath layers of dust in clerical libraries when they should be mandatory reading for insomniacs, the best sleeping-draft on the market, and no side-effects!

Once again Peter arrived almost half an hour late. It was most uncharacteristic of him, but I knew he had a lot on his plate.

"Now that I have briefly outlined the mystic way," he said, "let me come to the predicament in which you find yourself.

"Everybody who prays seriously and consistently for any length of time will eventually find themselves on the other side of first fervor, at the threshold of the night. This is the moment when the vast majority who come this far in prayer usually pack it all in — I know I nearly did. All my attempts at prayer were a complete failure. Each time I tried to pray in the way I once could I simply got nowhere. The Scriptures, the devotions, the meditations that moved me before moved me no more.

"Two tormentors always accompanied me to prayer. The first was a raking desire for God, the second was a mind full of distractions that drove me crazy, because I couldn't do anything about them. So my heart was restless, inside and outside the prayer that I thought was pointless. I was continually tempted to pack it all in and do something more constructive with my time."

"That's exactly how I've been feeling," I said, "and the truth is I have been making a run for it, but I don't seem to be getting very far because nothing satisfies me any more. I can't even get any pleasure out of the hobbies and the enthusiasms that used to excite me before."

"Right," said Peter. "All that you are saying confirms that you are on the right, not the wrong, path. In this strange new world in which you find yourself, it's as if you are caught between heaven and earth. Your heart wants to reach out and touch the love that has already touched you, but endless distractions vie with one another to draw you away from what you desperately desire. What you must now learn to do is to keep your heart's gaze fixed upon God, come hell or high water — nothing else matters. You can forget all the forms of prayer that helped you so much in the past, because they won't help you to continue in the future. Now you must learn to travel by contemplation, not by meditation.

"Let me introduce you to the prayer of the heart through a great mystical work called *The Cloud of Unknowing*. I'm sure you've come across it if you've not already read it."

"Yes," I said, "I have read it, but a long time ago, and I'm afraid it didn't mean much to me at the time."

"Well," said Peter, "let me explain very briefly its teaching on how to continue in prayer in the mystic way, because it makes a number of useful practical suggestions that will be of help to you. Speaking of the predicament in which you now find yourself, it says it's as if there is a 'cloud of unknowing' between you and your Maker that you cannot penetrate, at least at first. But no matter how difficult it may seem, you must nevertheless try to keep your heart's gaze fixed on the One who is hidden behind the cloud. Let your heart gaze upwards, as it were, with a 'naked intent,' without being clothed with any other desire, or without being distracted with any other thought that can hinder what it calls 'this work' that is more important than any other work.

"Now in order to keep this naked intent upon God who is hidden from view behind the cloud of unknowing, you must try to place a 'cloud of forgetfulness' between you and all and everything that would prevent you from gently trying to concentrate on God. All thought, all desires that would distract you in the slightest, must be covered over by this cloud of forgetfulness. It does not matter what they are — even if they are of God Himself, it says, and His holy angels — they will do you no good because they would only draw you away from 'this holy work.' They would only draw you away from the contemplation of God as He is in Himself to meditate on Him as you fashion Him for yourself. It is not too difficult to put what it calls holy and pious thoughts away, because, as you've already found, it's virtually impossible to pray or meditate as you could before anyway.

"However, there are other thoughts and desires that are more difficult to banish from your mind: the continual feeling that you are wasting your time, that this strange new form of prayer is pointless, that you'd be better employed doing something more practical. All these thoughts and feelings must not be countenanced, not for a single moment. They must all be put under the cloud of forgetfulness, so that they do not distract the naked intent upon God. With help and encouragement even these distractions can be put under the cloud, at least for a time, but then others rise up out of the depths and begin to burst through the cloud of forgetfulness to tantalize you, not just with distractions but with temptations. These temptations do not diminish but grow stronger and stronger as you continue. Past hurts and injuries rise up with such force and passion that they become all but irresistible. Before you realize what is happening you find yourself planning to get your own back, plotting revenge. You find yourself ripping other people's characters to pieces almost before you realize it. Powerful sensual and sexual feelings and desires erupt as if from nowhere. No matter how hard you try to keep putting these distractions under the cloud of forgetfulness, they keep reappearing as often as you would banish them."

"But if this is the case," I said, "wouldn't it be better to keep all these desires and temptations at bay by making a serious attempt to return to the sort of meditations that filled your mind before? Why not make a new effort to meditate again on Gospel scenes that depicted God's love in action and in words, speaking to us through all that Jesus said and did? Even if it were more difficult to do this than it was before, wouldn't it be preferable to submitting to these awful temptations and desires that will draw us away from the love we want to contemplate?"

"No, it wouldn't," said Peter, "and you couldn't do it even if you wanted to. This is the time for contemplation, not meditation. You see, in meditation you tried to gaze upon the love of God as it was literally embodied in Jesus and in everything that He said and did in the past. This was an important stage in your spiritual journey. It helped to strengthen and inspire the heart's desire that must now learn to gaze upon His love, not as it expressed itself in the past but as it is expressing itself now in the present.

"The good news which is the Gospel is not just that God's love was poured out in the past through Jesus, but that it is being poured out now in the present through Jesus who is risen from the dead and is alive at this moment in time and at every moment in time. This was the good news that Peter proclaimed on the first Pentecost day, when he himself had been so filled with the love of the Risen Christ that at first everyone thought he was drunk. Remember the scene — remember the sermon. The essence of it was this: the Jesus we all knew and loved, the One who was promised for generations by the prophets and who was crucified, is now alive again, and is pouring out the fullness of His love on all who would receive it.

"Those who heard what was being said and believed it were deeply moved, not least because they could see for themselves that Peter had already received what he was offering to others, so they said, 'What must we do?' Peter's answer was simply this, 'Repent, be baptized, have your sins forgiven and receive the gift of the Holy Spirit.' In other words turn your heart back to the God whose love is being poured out through the Risen One, and be baptized.

"There are two baptisms, one of water and one of fire. The first could be received immediately, so that they could be opened up to receive the second baptism of fire which would gradually purify them from all sin and selfishness. Then they would be able to receive the gift of the Holy Spirit, who would unite them perfectly with the Risen Christ. In Christian tradition, the mystic way is the place where the believer practices repentance as never before through the prayer of the heart until that heart is purified by the baptism of fire for the habitation of the Holy Spirit."

Only the day before, Peter had spoken to me about the touch of God that sometimes gave you a tingle down your spine and even brought out goose pimples to confirm you hadn't imagined it. That was happening to me as Peter was speaking. I'd never heard anything quite like it before. It was as if I were with the crowds on the first day of Pentecost, hearing the good news being proclaimed for the first time.

"Now," said Peter, "you've already been baptized by water, but you've yet to be baptized with fire. You have repented in a general way before, but now you must repent in a particular way again and again and again. In this strange new prayer you are in fact practicing repentance as often as you turn back to God from all that tries to turn you away from Him. The author of *The Cloud of Unknowing* is right. There is no more important work than this.

"Because it is such a difficult work, the author of *The Cloud* gives invaluable advice that will help you to keep turning to receive the self-same life and love that the Apostles received on the first day of Pentecost. He suggests taking a single word and then repeating it over and over again. It's a device that was used by the Desert Fathers. The words he suggests are not prayers in themselves, they are rather props to help keep the heart's attention fixed on God. He uses a medieval metaphor to make his point. He says the word that you choose to use will be like both a spear and a shield. The word acts like a shield when its repetition enables you to parry the distractions that cannot be stifled by the cloud of forgetfulness. Simultaneously it acts like a spear that is used to prop up, as it were, your naked intent upon God, so that it can pierce through the cloud of unknowing to the Godhead there in hiding. The words he suggests are: God, sin, love and lump. If they don't appeal to you, no matter — choose others that do. The words are not important in themselves, it's what they are used for that's important, and how they are used.

"What I'm going to suggest to you is a slightly different approach that I've found helpful myself. Instead of choosing a single word I started off by choosing a single sentence, one that I felt somehow summed up how I felt at the time, how I related or didn't relate to the God who seemed to have taken His leave of me. I chose the prayer Jesus Himself made upon the Cross, most especially when everything seemed too much, 'My God, my God, why have you forsaken me?' — or the prayer He made in Gethsemane, particularly when temptations came thick and fast, 'Father, that this chalice may be taken away from me.' When I felt really in the pits, I turned to the *De Profundis* — 'Out of the depths I cried to thee, O Lord; Lord, hear my prayer' — or the prayer from Cardinal Newman's famous hymn, 'Lead, kindly light, amidst the encircling gloom.' The Jesus Prayer, designed especially for this particular moment of the mystic way, is perhaps the best known of all — 'Jesus, Son of God, have mercy on me, a sinner.'

"At moments when I felt touched by the presence of God who'd seemed absent for so long, I turned to phrases of praise and thanksgiving to express how I felt; but that was not often, at least in the early stages. The important thing is to choose something that genuinely embodies how you feel at the time. It's no good pretending with God. He knows exactly how you feel anyway — it's no good trying to soft-soap Him. What's important to remember is that these phrases are only used to keep helping you turn back to God from the distractions that would turn you away from Him. Don't try to dwell on them or intellectually inspect them. They're not to help you to meditate, but to contemplate.

"Now, please don't feel you've got to choose what appealed to me: choose phrases you feel appeal to you, but use them in the way I suggest to help you to keep repenting. What I found, and what you'll find, is that in time the full sentence will be too long, and you'll feel the need to reduce it to, say, just 'My God, my God' or 'Out of the depths' or 'Lead, kindly light' or 'Have mercy on me, a sinner.' Then the time will come when you'll be back to where we started with the cloud of unknowing, when a single word will be all you need. Like 'God,' or 'Jesus,' or 'mercy.' I can't give you rules when to change down from many to few, you'll know for yourself. It's like changing gears in a car, once you get used to using them you know automatically when to change down. Some people like to count the words or the phrases on beads — it's not necessary, but if it helps to keep gently fixing your gaze on God, that's all that matters.

"These suggestions are not prayer but aids to prayer, the prayer of the heart where repentance is learned better than anywhere else. This repentance of heart that is practiced in the darkness is worth ten times what is practiced in the light. It's easy to pray when the well is full and brimming over, but it's far more difficult to pray when the well runs dry.

"This is why it is of paramount importance to give exactly the same time to prayer that you gave when prayer was full of feeling and fervor, so that you can show by the very consistency of your daily presence that you are prepared to go on giving even when you seem to receive nothing in return. Anyone can give when they are receiving in return, but only a mature adult can go on giving in pure selfless love when their love seems to be received with indifference, if it seems to be received at all. This is what my parents had to learn when their well ran dry and what everyone must learn if they are to get anywhere in the spiritual life.

"Now you can see the real meaning of the strange spiritual

desert in which you find yourself. It is the place where you offer yourself to God through a process of daily repentance as you endeavor to raise your mind and heart to Him through selfless loving. It is a loving that will always be returned in kind whether it is the kind of love that purifies in turmoil and strife or in peace and tranquillity. God will do His part if we do ours. Our part is to keep on gently turning to Him again and again, keep on raising our hearts whether they feel empty or whether they feel full.

"If you persevere, the time will come when the action of God's love will begin to draw you into an ever-deepening Recollection or Quiet or even Full Union. Then you will find less and less need for any of the forms of prayer that supported you along the way. All you'll want to do is to remain still and gaze in awe-filled silence upon the One whom you feel drawing you onward into the peace that surpasses all understanding.

"Now, these suggestions that I've made are like the oars on a boat that you use to guide it downriver towards the sea. At first you have to row hard to get the boat moving towards its destination, but when the momentum has been built up you can sit back and rest for a while as it moves silently forward. The moment the boat starts to slow down, drifts towards the bank or gets caught in a cross-current, then you have to start rowing again to keep it moving in the right direction. And so you keep journeying on, at one moment rowing to keep the boat on course, at another resting, enjoying the surrounding countryside. As you approach the sea you need to row less and less, as you experience the pull of the tide drawing you onwards. Once you have left the river you can put aside the oars and set up the sails. Now you can travel with ease and with speed, with the tide on your side and the wind in your sails; another power takes over to do for you what you could never do for yourself."

"That sounds wonderful," I said.

"Does it?" said Peter. "Have you ever done any sailing?"

"No, I haven't."

"I thought not," said Peter. "If you had, you'd know it's not all plain sailing when you put out to sea. The weather can change in an instant, no matter what the forecasters have promised, and you can find yourself at the wrong end of a force eight or worse in a matter of minutes."

Peter was smiling but I took his point. I knew it wouldn't be all plain sailing ahead. Although I was only a beginner in the strange new world that had led me to ask for Peter's help once more, I knew enough to know that Peter was a complete master of his subject. He was not only able to explain the mystic way with a unique simplicity, but he was able to integrate it into an authentic biblical spirituality with ease and facility. I'd always been led to believe that the mystic way was an obscure, eccentric and esoteric way for a few chosen souls, whom you may admire from a distance but whom you would follow at your peril. I remember the first spiritual director I ever had shaking his finger at me and saying, "Beware of mysticism. It always begins in mist and ends in schism!"

Peter had made everything that I had initially thought strange, so ordinary, so commonplace, so part and parcel of a normal Christian response to the Gospel.

"Thank you so much for explaining everything so clearly," I said. "I only wish everyone could hear how you've explained everything to me. Then I'm sure many more would be encouraged to go on in prayer beyond first beginning, not only priests and religious, but even lay people too."

Peter started laughing. "Have I said something funny?" I said.

"No, not really," Peter said, pulling himself together. "I'm sorry, it was just the way you said, 'even lay people' that made me laugh. You see I believe far more lay people and far more married people than you would ever imagine journey on to the heights of mystical prayer though they don't even know it. Take my mother as a case in point. She never studied theology and the Bible was literally a closed book to her and her generation for reasons we well know, but that does not mean she was deprived of the Gospel. Nor did anyone instruct her in mystical theology, but I'll wager she knew more about the mystic way than either of us, in the only way that really matters."

"How do you mean?" I asked.

"Well," said Peter, "she had a great devotion to the Sacred Heart all her life. It was a devotion that she tried to hand on to me when I was a small boy. We used to have a large picture of the Sacred Heart on the wall halfway up the stairs. When she found me looking at it one morning she told me who the Sacred Heart was and what the flames around His heart meant. I remember pointing my finger at the picture and saying, 'It's Mr. Loving!' The whole family burst out laughing when they were told of the first theological statement I ever made. I couldn't work out why everybody was laughing at me. I remember saying to myself, 'Why is everyone laughing at me? He is Mr. Loving, He is — I know it.' Years later when I studied philosophy I found that I was right. Aristotle said that God is 'Pure Act.' That means He is what He does, and He does what He is. In other words, He is not just love, but He is loving, and He is loving all the time. All this was reconfirmed later when I studied Scripture.

"However, I have to admit I became something of a spiritual snob when I began to study theology in Paris at the time of the Second Vatican Council. I began to look down on the simple spirituality I'd been brought up on, and my artistic sensibilities were offended by some of those ghastly statues of the Sacred Heart that were to be found in our churches, and the awful paintings of Him that most Catholics hung with pride in their homes. For years I studied the liturgical movement. The Paschal Mystery became the center of my spirituality. I began to understand the meaning and importance of the Resurrection as never before. It was not just a great historical event that took place two thousand years ago, it was an event that is happening now. Jesus is risen now. He is alive now, and the same power, the same love that raised Him from the dead, is accessible now to all who receive it, to do in us what has already been done in Him.

"It took me many more years to realize that, as T.S. Eliot

wrote, 'The end of all our journeying is to end up at the place where we started and to know that place for the first time.' The wonderful truths that I'd learned from my study of the new theology weren't new at all. I'd been brought up on them, as had my parents and their parents before them. The plaster statues of 'Mr. Loving' might be a little old-fashioned by today's standards, and the pictures that used to be so common in our homes may not be as acceptable today as they were in the past, but the truth behind the devotion to the Sacred Heart is the most important truth of our faith. That truth is timeless. Who is the Sacred Heart but Jesus risen from the dead? He is not just represented as love incarnate but as incarnate loving. He is Mr. Loving.

"After years of studying theology and traveling all over Europe in search of wisdom, I came home to find that my mother had known before I left all that was necessary for the journey I still hadn't begun. While I'd spent years searching for the point of departure, she'd been traveling relentlessly on and on ahead of me, with such simplicity and humility that contrasted so unfavorably with the arrogance of her son. I didn't learn anything about her prayer life at the time, I was too busy reading about everyone else's — studying the Christian mystical tradition, from the Desert Fathers to Saint John of the Cross and beyond. It was only when I paid a short visit home after living alone in the Outer Hebrides for about ten years that I found out how she'd been praying over the years, how she'd been responding to Mr. Loving, and what had led her onwards to the higher reaches of the mystic way."

Peter paused as he began to search through his pockets for something. But I was unable to contain my impatience, so I said, "And what was it that led her to the heights?" I was hoping to hear of some short cut.

"It was these," said Peter, taking a small leather case out of his breast pocket. He opened it and took out a tiny pair of golden rosary beads. He could see I was disappointed.

"Don't be disappointed," he said. "These beads have led countless generations of people to the heights of mystical prayer without them ever realizing it. It is a magnificent method of prayer, because it contains within it every method of prayer that is necessary to lead a person on to the heights of contemplation. To begin with, a person may just say the individual prayers as best they can; then they may move on to meditation on the mysteries of Christ's life that will lead them eventually to the high point of Adolescent Prayer. And when they are led beyond, they will learn, as my mother did, how to use the rosary to sustain them through the dark nights ahead of them, how to help keep their hearts and minds fixed upon God with naked intent, when He seems to have hidden Himself in the cloud of unknowing.

"I had come home to visit my mother because she was ill and confined to bed. When I visited her in her room she always had these beads in her hand. When I asked her about the rosary, she said almost apologetically that she could no longer say it as she once could, she found it quite impossible. All she did was to take a word from the 'Our Father,' the 'Hail Mary' or the 'Glory Be' and say it slowly and prayerfully. It might be just the phrase 'Glory be to God,' or 'Thy will be done,' or simply the word 'Jesus.' Then, she said, she sometimes didn't say anything at all for hours on end. She just wanted to be there with God. She wasn't very forthcoming when I asked her to describe what happened in those moments. I realized I'd gone too far, asking her to talk about something that was obviously too personal and too profound. When I went back to Barra I thanked God for the mother He'd given me, and for the example of someone who was far more advanced than me. I'd traveled all over the globe searching for wisdom that I could have found in my own home and from my own mother, had I but a fraction of the humility I'd found in her."

Peter was on his feet. "Well, I suppose I'd better be on my way," he said.

"Thank you again, Peter," I said as I led him to the door. "Oh, one final problem, I'm afraid. I feel you've still got a lot to say to me but I have to leave tomorrow evening to be back in time for the weekend."

"Oh dear," said Peter. "I hadn't realized it was Friday today. But don't worry. I think I can come for the whole day tomorrow because my brother David arrives tonight, and he will want to spend some time with my father tomorrow. He had to dash off immediately after the funeral as he was in the middle of giving a retreat in London."

"Are you sure?" I said.

"Positive," said Peter. "But I'll have to impose on you for lunch if that's all right."

"No problem at all," I said. I'd been living out of tins since I arrived, so the prospect of taking Peter out to lunch appealed to me immensely.

6

I had packed and was ready to leave by the time Peter arrived, shortly after nine o'clock. I didn't want to waste a minute of the day ahead. I was so intent on using every second of my last day with Peter that I didn't even enquire about his father, or whether or not his brother David had arrived the evening before. Peter had hardly time to sit down before I began.

"Peter," I said, "I've been so lucky finding you. You've been able to explain everything to me so simply that I know without a shadow of a doubt that I am on the right path. But what about others who think that the end of their first fervor is the end of their prayer life? How can they be helped when there are so few people who understand the mystic way as you do?"

"Well, I must admit," said Peter, "I didn't find anyone to help me in my years of solitude. If it hadn't been for Saint John of the Cross I think I'd have packed up prayer years ago. I didn't know what was happening to me until I read the signs that Saint John describes in his *Dark Night* that convinced me that I was after all on the right path.

"It's so important to have some clear guidelines, because anyone can have dryness and aridity in their prayer and everyone can suffer from distractions, but it doesn't automatically mean that they are in the dark night. A misinterpretation could set them back by encouraging them to persevere in a way of prayer that would be quite unsuited to them."

"Where do you find these classic signs?" I asked.

"In two places," said Peter. "In *The Dark Night of the Soul,* book one, chapter nine, and in *The Ascent of Mount Carmel,* book two, chapter thirteen."

"That's interesting. I didn't realize that," I said, "and I was only reading *The Dark Night* the other evening before I went to bed. What exactly are the signs?"

"Well," said Peter, "you can read them for yourself. He gives three or possibly four signs, but there are others that he assumes, and still others that you can find in the writings of other mystics. I've mentioned most of them already, so I'll be brief. There are about ten altogether.

"The first sign I would look for is that a person has already gone through their first fervor, as you have done, when meditation leading to what I call acquired contemplation becomes relatively easy. Then, after enjoying a sort of emotional climax for a relatively short time, everything suddenly flops into an anti-climax, when all the feelings of fervor disappear and do not return despite all one's efforts to revive them. This can happen to a person in their private prayer, or in forms of group prayer such as that experienced by people in the charismatic movement. However, I'd just like to say in passing that people who do not pray daily and consistently will not pass through their first fervor and into the mystic way, whether they pray mainly in private or whether they pray as members of a particular prayer group. Spiritual dilettantes and dabblers can play around with their emotions for a lifetime, misusing them to generate the requisite religious feeling when it suits them, or when they happen to be in the mood. These people will get nowhere beyond the next emotional high.

"Many unfortunates who get caught up in dubious religious sects have their emotions ruthlessly exploited at prescribed spiritual 'potboilers' that are held to keep the troops on a permanent high and firmly in the hands of their exploiters. Naturally these people do not progress on an authentic spiritual journey because they are not on one. While they may think and feel that they are, they are sadly in the hands of others with hidden agendas that have little to do with God and His Kingdom, but everything to do with their own. However, I digress.

"The second sign is, and this is mentioned by Saint John, that despite the restlessness, the aridity and the dryness, there is a deep desire for God that grows if they press on. The desire expresses itself in a pull to be alone that relentlessly draws them aside into solitude for the contemplative prayer that they want above all else, but which always seems to elude them.

"The third sign is that, despite the desire that regularly draws them to prayer, they find it all but impossible to concentrate as they did before. The reason is quite simple. As the heart's desire or the will is drawn to God alone it loses its power over the mind, the memory and the imagination, that were so essential for the meditation that now becomes quite impossible.

"The fourth sign is that, as their inner sensual faculties cannot function as they could before, they cannot picture the Jesus who was the center of their Adolescent Prayer, so their desire is directed towards God and God alone. Henceforward He is the only One who gradually becomes the object of their deepest desires and longings, although the experience of His Presence seems to have totally left them.

"The fifth sign is that the lack of concentration that afflicts them inside prayer begins to affect them outside prayer also. They moon around like lost souls, not knowing where to go or where to look for the love that they have lost. Like anyone who is in love with love, they become vague, woolly, dreamy and forgetful. The pleasures, pastimes, the interests, the hobbies, as well as their work, leave them flat. They find it difficult to concentrate on anything except this strange desire for God. The paradox is that they no longer have any interest even in the sacraments, or the liturgy, or in reading the Scriptures that meant so much to them before, or in devotional exercises or the hymns that helped them in the past. It's not surprising, then, that they begin to doubt that this strange new world in which they find themselves has anything to do with God after all.

"The sixth sign is that they appear to be suffering from a moral decline that they cannot stem. They seem to be getting worse rather than better. The truth of the matter is that the spiritual fervor that they were able to generate before no longer sustains their moral behavior, and they seem to be going backwards and unable to do anything about it. But the situation is not as serious as it seems. It's just that the sweet vapors of first fervor had hidden from view what was always lurking beneath the surface.

"The seventh sign is that certain temptations always tend to predominate at the beginning of the night of the senses. The temptation to pack up prayer permanently becomes at times almost irresistible, because it seems that they are going nowhere at all. It all seems to be a waste of time, doing nothing day after day in the time that used to be full of such wonderful feelings and fervor. The vast majority usually succumb, and never go any further in their prayer life. As they cannot return to Adolescent Prayer, they can only return to Juvenile Prayer if they pray much at all. If, however, a person does persevere, the temptations only increase, and their failure to find any sort of pleasure where it was found once before leads a person to seek it elsewhere. So they are beset with sensual and sexual temptations, inside and outside prayer, to which they succumb regularly, making it even more difficult for them to believe that they can be on any sort of spiritual journey.

"These temptations, and others that I will talk about later, get worse as the night of the senses gives way to the night of the spirit. It's no wonder that the eighth sign is depression. Not chronic or acute depression. That comes later! — just common or garden variety depression. Who wouldn't get depressed when it seems that you can't pray any more, and the Scriptures that meant so much to you before move you no longer, and your moral behavior seems to be deteriorating with each passing day. What's worse, other people seem to be noticing it too, and they see yesterday's happy, smiling 'saint in the making' making a mockery of his perseverance in prayer by persevering in liverish and bilious behavior that seems to belie a genuine spiritual journey. But worse still, it seems that nothing can be done about it.

"The ninth sign is that if, despite everything, a person does persevere in prayer come what may, all the negative features that have been outlined above will get progressively worse — at least for a time! It's not surprising, therefore, that the final sign is that they will eventually be totally convinced that they are on the wrong path. And if they are ever lucky enough to find a spiritual director who does understand them, then they will spend much of their time trying to convince their director that they are indeed on the wrong path.

"If all the above signs cannot be verified simultaneously, then it's a sure sign that the difficulties in prayer that present themselves do not signify that a person has arrived at the threshold of the dark night. If, despite all I've said, it's still impossible to make a diagnosis with certainty, the person should only be encouraged to practice the prayer forms usually prescribed for people in the night if all other forms of prayer have been tried and failed."

"Thank you so much, Peter," I said. "If I've ever doubted you before, I doubt you no more. These signs explain perfectly my present predicament. They also explain why prayer has been ten times more difficult than it ever was. But there's something that I'm still not clear about — it's about the Scriptures. I may have got it all wrong, but I got the impression that once Adolescent Prayer comes to an end and Adult Prayer begins you don't use the Scriptures any more, and the humanity of Jesus no longer seems to have the importance it had before."

"Good," said Peter. "I'm glad that you've raised the point. Now, it's not that the humanity of Jesus has disappeared, it's just that, as you put it, it *seems* to have disappeared.

"In spiritual adolescence, the Scriptures were a window through which you could see Jesus Christ and study everything that He said and did. He was the fulfillment of all your hopes and dreams, but you gazed upon Him from the outside like an onlooker or a bystander. All that has changed now. Once an outsider is touched by love, he wants to be an insider. Love wants to reach out, to take hold of, it wants to possess, it wants to enter into, it wants at-one-ment with the one who is loved. The mystic way begins precisely because the heart's deepest longings and desires outreach everything else for the intimate and personal at-one-ment that is the be-all and end-all of all authentic loving.

"It reminds me of the story of the astronaut who'd been chosen to pilot one of the first spaceships to the Moon with his best friend. Every day he woke up to see the spaceship that was going to carry him to his destination. It was the fulfillment of all his hopes and dreams, for which he had given the best years of his life. Every morning he woke up feeling wonderful, full of life and energy for the day ahead, for the final preparation for lift-off. Then one morning he awoke feeling awful. His mouth was dry, his body was cramped and he had an almighty headache, and he could see nothing. 'It's gone! It's gone, the spaceship has gone!' he shouted. Then he heard the voice of his friend through the intercom. 'No it hasn't,' he said. 'You can't see it because you're in it.' And he *was* in it, and he was traveling more quickly than ever before towards the destination that he believed he had been born for.

"You can no longer see Jesus as you used to because you are within Him and are being fitted into Him more perfectly in your prayer than ever before. If you gently try to journey on in Him, with Him and through Him, then you will travel far faster than when you were just a bystander. Nor have the Scriptures to be set aside. You may not be able to use them in prayer as you did in the past, but you must study them outside prayer more assiduously than ever because they must be your main inspiration and guide. Now, however, you will read and understand them in a new light, in the light of your most recent experience in the mystic way. You'll want to know more clearly just where you are going, and how you are going to get there.

"When you study Jesus in His resurrection life you'll see Him as He is now, and how He is acting now to draw you ever more deeply into Himself. When you study Him in His earthly life you see Him as He was, but you'll also see how He acted then to respond to the same love that is drawing you now. You're rather like a young mountaineer preparing to scale the heights. The Master Mountaineer has already gone before you and He is beckoning you to follow Him, but you won't be able to do so unless you have studied the way He climbed ahead of you. This is why you must study how Jesus reacted in His prayer life to the same love that you are beginning to experience in yours.

"So let's look at the Scriptures for a moment to see what light they can shed on Jesus's personal prayer life, because the way He prayed will be the best of all guides to how you should pray. We don't know anything about His personal prayer life before He began to appear in public, and we might never have known how He prayed then if He hadn't gone out of His way to tell us. There were no witnesses when He prayed alone in the desert, and those who were there in Gethsemane were by all accounts asleep, so He must have considered it of utmost importance to tell someone later, so that everyone could know about it. If you reread these important accounts of Jesus at prayer you'll be astounded by how similar His prayer was to your own.

"Whether it was in the desert at the beginning of His public life or in Gethsemane at the end of it, you'll see Him battling against powerful distractions and temptations that would turn His heart's attention from the Father's love that drew Him into solitude in the first place. In short, you'll see Him practicing the prayer of the heart like so many mystics who followed Him. Reread the account of Jesus at prayer in the garden of Gethsemane and you'll see what I mean. You'll see Him choosing a short prayer that He repeats to help Him parry the distractions that assail Him, while helping Him to keep His heart's attention on God. His prayer is remarkably honest and sums up His heart's deepest desire: 'Father, that this chalice may be taken away from me; yet not my will, but Your will be done.' Perhaps that's the best prayer of all when the darkness gathers around us and terrible temptations threaten to turn us away from the path ahead."

"I see," I said. "So I suppose you could say that Jesus is practicing the repentance in His prayer that I have to practice in mine.

"That's right," said Peter. "That's why the prayer that you were beginning to think had no meaning at all is in fact the prayer that enables you to pray in harmony with His prayer."

"Thank you," I said. "Everything is becoming clearer all the time. So when we respond to Saint Peter's call to repent, by trying to repent repeatedly in our daily prayer, we are doing exactly what Jesus did in His prayer."

"Yes!" said Peter. "But you've left something out, something rather important that makes a difference, a big difference. What Saint Peter actually said was that you must repent to have your sins forgiven, and then you would receive the gift of the Holy Spirit. Jesus did not need to repent to have His sins forgiven. He may have repented because He turned away from temptation, but He was never a penitent because He never sinned. But we're penitents because we *have* sinned and we *do* sin, and that's why the baptism of fire that we have to undergo entails confronting not just evil in general but the evil that is within all of us but was never in Him. He may have been surrounded by the power of Evil that assailed Him from the outside, but we are also assailed by the power of Evil from the inside.

"Nevertheless, you can see that your prayer is now all but identical with the prayer of Jesus. When you go to pray now it's like going into the desert with Him, and sometimes it will be like going into Gethsemane with Him. But remember, however hard, however difficult your prayer may become, you are performing the most sacred action possible to man!"

I couldn't help laughing. "You mean you're trying to tell me that when I spend hours struggling against distractions and temptations I've been performing the most sacred action possible to man?"

"Yes, I do," said Peter. He wasn't laughing, he was in deadly earnest. "Remember the words of the great penitential psalm that makes it quite clear that the gift God wants, the sacrifice He desires above all else, is that of a pure, humble and contrite heart. This is the offering that you are trying to make in harmony with the offering that Jesus made in His prayer.

"When we are baptized we are baptized not just into Christ's life but into His action, into His priestly action, where we try to make the same offering that He made. His offering is perfect because His heart is pure. Ours isn't; indeed, our hearts are far from being pure. That's why although we pray in harmony with Him, we do not pray in complete conformity with Him. The Holy Spirit has been sent and is being sent so that the first baptism of water that enabled us to enter into His Priestly Prayer will be brought to perfection by the baptism of fire. Then, when we have been purified we will be able to pray in complete conformity with Him.

"Christ's Priestly Prayer is pure and perfect because it is totally untainted by the sin that soils and sullies our prayer. The whole point and purpose of the baptism of fire that purifies and refines our love in the dark night is to unite it to Christ's love at the end of it. Then the Holy Spirit, who made us in the image of Christ to begin with, will make us into His likeness to end with. A likeness not just in being but in acting, as we are transformed perfectly into His priestly action, when we can finally offer the same gift, the same sacrifice, the same offering — a pure and perfect heart."

Peter paused for a few moments to let what he had been saying sink in before he continued.

"So you see," he said, "far from being separated from the humanity of Jesus in the mystic way, you are closer to it than ever before, because it is the way for those who want to enter into it ever more fully. It is the way for those who want to share not just in Christ's human being but in His human action — in His priestly action.

"Now, the Scriptures that were once studied only superficially can eventually be studied at far greater depths, and shed light where little light was shed before. Deeper insights and profounder understandings endow the traveler on the mystic way with a wisdom that is quite inaccessible to the spiritual adolescent. I purposely use the word 'eventually,' because to begin with and for some considerable time the ever-deepening darkness of the night prevents travelers from seeing anything to their spiritual advantage in the Scriptures, or anywhere else for that matter. That's why spiritual directors can be of paramount importance, because they give meaning to the travelers who can't find it for themselves anywhere at all, as I have been trying to do for you.

"My own mother was a case in point. She was fortunate that she could turn to her friend Gus when everything became too much for her in her dark night. He helped her most of all at her midnight hour when she had to suffer more than she had ever suffered before. He gave meaning where there seemed to be no meaning at all. It all happened when my eldest brother James announced that he wanted to become a priest. It wasn't just that, but he wanted to become a Cistercian priest. That meant that once he left home he would never return. Naturally my mother was totally bereft. She was proud that her son wanted to be a priest, but why did he want to become a monk as well? She didn't know what to do, but fortunately she did have Gus to turn to.

"He told her that a mother only really fulfills and completes her motherhood when her love is so great that she allows her child to both choose and follow his own chosen vocation in life, whatever that may mean. He told her that this was the sacrifice that Mary had to make when she had to allow the Son to whom she'd given birth to go His own way and to respond to the vocation that He was called to. My mother felt much better after talking to Gus — after all, he was a priest and a monk himself, and so he was able to console and encourage her better than anyone else.

"Then my brother had a terrible accident on the way to his final examinations. He slipped down the stairs on the underground, hit his head and was killed instantly. He was only twenty-two. I was still at school and was called out of study to be told of the tragedy. When I got home it was to find my mother all but inconsolable. She'd already come to terms with the sacrifice that she'd been asked to make when he chose to become a monk; now she was asked to make another, a more complete and final sacrifice that she'd never thought for a moment would ever be asked of her.

"Once again she turned to Gus for spiritual help. He told her that she was now being asked to be the priest that James never became. He told her that the first priest after Christ Himself had been a woman and a mother, and that the greatest sacrifice that she had had to make was the sacrifice of her own Son. All Mary's life had revolved around selflessly giving her all for the Son she bore. Everything had always been for Him. And then she had to give absolutely everything, even Him. This was the most perfect and complete sacrifice any mother has ever had to make, and she made it standing there at the foot of the Cross.

"My mother never forgot what Gus said to her. It didn't take away all the pain, but it did give meaning to it and made it bearable. What helped most was seeing that the sacrifice she had to make was exactly the sacrifice Mary made, with and through her own Son on Calvary. She saw that the realization of her priesthood was as terrifyingly real. She was not only asked to offer her heart and mind in prayer, but her grief-stricken body too, in and out of prayer, and the first, most precious fruit of that body. The painful sacrifice that my mother had to make in the darkest moment of her dark night did not tempt her to abandon her priesthood, but to embrace it more fully for the rest of her life.

"She'd always made a morning offering, ever since she was a little girl, but suddenly that offering had a new meaning. It was now the key moment in her day, when she expressed in prayer the priestly offering that would be lived out in the rest of her day as she sacrificed herself for her children, for her husband and for anyone who had need of what she had to give. In the end, her morning offering was not a lengthy prayer as it had been to begin with, but just a short phrase or a few words like the words Christ had used in Gethsemane or on Calvary — words that would be recalled and repeated at odd moments of the day to remind her of the priestly nature of her role as wife and mother. This was how she understood and exercised her prayer of the heart that consecrated all she said and all she did.

"It was from my mother that I first learned that the priestly offering of the heart and mind that is turned and opened to God inside prayer has to be put into practice outside prayer. It is here that the heart, the mind, the body and the whole person surrender themselves again and again to Him in the neighbor in need, as Christ had done. I learned this, not just from what my mother said, but from what I saw her do, day in, day out, for her own family and for the wider family of all who had needs that she could in some way satisfy."

Peter paused again, not for me this time but for himself, as he remembered the mother that he had just lost and all she had been to him.

"The last time I spoke to her about prayer," said Peter, "she told me that the morning offering that was once one among many prayers became virtually the only prayer, because it summed up all others. She discovered for herself that, no matter where you begin, the life of prayer always leads to the same place. It's the place where you turn and open yourself to the God to whom you totally surrender yourself as Christ had done. Any means of prayer that leads to this prayer of total surrender, of complete sacrifice, is genuine and authentic. Any words that are used at this supreme moment of prayer on earth are secondary to the inner attitude of heart and mind that ultimately needs no words. When this moment comes it's as if the total surrender of heart and mind to God is caught up in a sort of suspended animation. These moments of prayer without words are brief to begin with, and need sustaining by words until a pure heart and mind wills 'the one thing necessary' where and when 'silence reigns supreme.'

"This is the point in the journey into God where everybody

is ultimately united, whether they are Jews or whether they are Christians, whether they are Buddhists or whether they are Hindus, whether they are Muslims or whether they are Sufis. No matter what different prayer forms they may use to begin with or which support them along the way, all will be led to the still and silent gaze upon God in an inner attitude of total surrender.

"Christian mystics have used the simile of Jacob's Ladder to both describe and explain what happens at this supreme moment of prayer. The ladder symbolizes the heart or the will when it is caught up in this attitude of total surrender before God. The angels who constantly descend and ascend represent the Power of God, descending into man and rising up again bearing the little man has to offer in return. This is the prayer that ultimately facilitates a profound exchange of love, enabling the Power of God, the Holy Spirit, to begin the baptism of fire that will eventually bring about the forgiveness of sin that heralds the mystical indwelling of the divine in the human.

"When our priestly sacrifice is totally united with the priestly sacrifice of Christ, we are not only at one with what He offers but with what He receives in return. The end of all sacrifice is union, communion, at-one-ment. First atonement, then at-one-ment. That's why Jesus said He came for sinners, to seek them out and bring them the inner healing of heart, mind and body that would enable them to be at one with Him, with His human being and His human acting; then they could receive all He received until they were one with Him as He is one with the Father, one in heart, one in mind and one in body.

"When Christ healed people physically it was because He cared for them. But He made it clear that there was a more important form of healing that was symbolized by His physical healing. It was a spiritual healing that could not be seen but which must precede the close and intimate union that He wanted to have with all men and with all women. While He was on earth, this spiritual healing was limited by His physical body that could only be at one place at a time, with one person or group of persons at a time. But once raised from the dead He was no longer limited by a physical body, so He could reach out to touch the sick of every generation at the same time because He could do it from the inside, through the Holy Spirit.

"Now the One who once called Himself the Physician has sent another, a Consultant, who specializes in inner healing, the inner healing of all who would receive Him. It is the Perfect Psychiatrist, the Holy Spirit. He is the Perfect Psychiatrist because He is able to heal people not only of psychological abnormalities that prevent them entering fully into human life, but also of spiritual abnormalities that prevent them from entering fully into Christ's life.

"Now He works most perfectly in the night when, despite all the distractions and temptations that abound, the spiritually sick try as best they can to turn and open themselves to admit Him so that He can bring about their inner transformation. If there was no sin in us the transformation would be instant, as it was for Mary. Her total purity of heart meant that the moment she was touched by the Holy Spirit, the Christ Child was instantly conceived within her. But not so with us. We are not 'full of grace' and sin is so deeply imbedded within us that it is rock-solid. Instant transformation, therefore, is impossible. It will take very many years of painful healing therapy in the night under the influence of the Perfect Psychiatrist before sin's power can be destroyed, and we can be fully transformed into Christ.

"When I was a young man, I met a physicist in Italy, called Antonio. He'd given up a prestigious academic career to become a hermit in the hills above Borgo San Sepolcro. I learned as much about the spiritual life from him as from anyone else I've ever met. He said that, at the beginning of the inner purification, the Holy Spirit strikes us as an irresistible force, meeting the sin that is so deeply imbedded within us as an immovable object. He reminded me of what happens when an irresistible force strikes an immovable object. At first nothing happens, there's an impasse. Then, if neither gives way, the combined effect of an irresistible force on an immovable object generates heat. This is the beginning of the baptism of fire, when the Holy Spirit, the Perfect Psychiatrist, begins His work of purifying us as we pray until we are so pure that we can be fully integrated into the pure and perfect Priestly Prayer of Christ."

Peter paused for a moment, gazing at nothing in particular on the floor in front of him before standing up.

"Now," he said, "I think it's time to look at the psychology behind the symbolism to see precisely what it is that facilitates mystical transformation. But first, let's have a cup of coffee! I know I've already said a lot, but I've got so much more to say before you leave this evening."

Peter didn't waste any **7** time. As soon as we'd had our coffee he immediately began where we'd left off.

"Now," he said, "in order to explain why a person needs purification in the dark night, Saint John of the Cross details the typical faults and failings of beginners in first fervor. The funny thing is that when a person is busy playing the part of a would-be saint they are usually quite blind to what others around them can see quite clearly. Shakespeare said that all the world's a stage and the men and women merely players, each playing their part. Nobody wants to see themselves as they really are, let alone have others see what they can't face for themselves. So we pass through life as if on a stage, playing a chosen part and posturing to make ourselves acceptable to those who we feel wouldn't otherwise accept us.

"Nobody must be allowed to see what is below the surface, what is under the stage. The trapdoor to the grim and grimy underworld must be kept closed at all times. The truth of the matter is that despite all our play-acting we are in fact determined by what we try at all times to keep locked away below-stage in our unconscious. Sometimes what's called a 'Freudian slip' takes place, when something is revealed that we have been trying to keep hidden away, not only from others but even from ourselves. Then the real cause of what has been dressed up as rational human behavior suddenly springs out from below-stage, from the unconscious, before we have time to put our foot on the trapdoor.

In an instant we stand exposed for what we are before the audience we were trying to impress the moment before.

"It happened to me in a rather dramatic way in the late sixties. I received a letter from my brother Tony, who was then a missionary in South Africa, to say that he was not only leaving the Order but getting married. My parents received a similar letter, but no mention was made of his desire to get married. They were so upset that they decided to go and see him and they asked me to go with them. The family came together at a little place called Piet Retief in the Transvaal, where he was the parish priest. My brother didn't beat about the bush. He told us immediately not only that he was going to leave the Order and the priesthood, but that he intended to get married in the near future.

"Naturally my parents were shocked when he actually told them, but they were in no way prepared for what came next. He told them he was going to marry a black African, a Zulu, whom he had met at one of the mission stations. They were shattered and said so. You can imagine all that they said on the spur of the moment; the racism that they had no knowledge of came pouring out. The atmosphere in the room was electric. I sat there as the still and silent center amidst all the turmoil, and I said not a word. But I was horrified at what was happening within me. Everything that my parents were saying out loud I was saying to myself. Everything happened so quickly that I had no time to put my foot on the trapdoor. The racism that I had never dreamt was in me came up and flooded my mind. I managed to close it quickly before anything more could come out, and managed to close my mouth too, so that nobody would know that what was in my parents was also in me.

"I didn't sleep that night. I'd been shattered to the roots of my being — there'd been an evil spiritual cancer within me for years and I didn't even know it. I'd been the president of the Anti-Apartheid League at college. I'd spoken out and written about the pernicious disease of racism. I'd demonstrated time and time again in Trafalgar Square in front of the South African Embassy, and all the time I'd been one of them myself. But that wasn't all that kept me awake that night — it was the thought of all the other prejudices that were harbored deep down within me, determining for the worse the man I thought I'd known so well but who had suddenly become a stranger to me.

"I knew then, and I knew for sure, that I had been prejudiced against black Africans. I knew it must have shown in the raucous way I'd demonstrated for them, and in the patronizing way I'd treated them. And yet I hadn't seen it, I hadn't even dreamt it could be possible, and I would have reacted violently to anyone who suggested otherwise. Just how many other prejudices lurked deep down within me — that was the question I asked myself as I tossed and turned my way through the night. How much of the behavior of the man I thought I knew was determined by another man, what Saint Paul called the 'Old Man,' who had homed himself deep down within me? Then I thought of the enormous pride that had blinded me to the truth. I'd not only managed to deceive others, I'd deceived myself about the real quality of the man who had the audacity to think he was a 'saint in the making' just because he had religious pretensions that were probably born of some pride or prejudice of which he had no knowledge.

"That night was the moment of truth in my life. Now I could see as never before that the man who'd been playing the would-be saint on his own little stage to his chosen audience was a fraud, a fake, a phony. He was ruled from deep down within by the pride and prejudice of the 'Old Man' — he was his creature, though he hadn't known it. I think the worst realization of all was that even though I could see so clearly what I'd never been able to see before, there was nothing I could do about it.

"I felt so helpless. I knew that I, the great moral crusader, was a racist and I could do nothing to change myself. I remember a therapist who used to lecture in psychology at teachers' training college, explaining how once the cause of irrational behavior had been discovered in the unconscious mind and shown to the sufferer in the conscious mind they would be cured of their affliction. I thought he was wrong at the time. Now I know that he was wrong. I was a racist although I'd not known it, and the mere fact that I knew what I didn't know before didn't change me at all.

"I remember wandering through the streets of Johannesburg, looking at black African women and trying to imagine my brother married to one of them. I simply couldn't, nor could I do anything to free myself from the racism that had me in its power. How could I possibly be cured? It was only after they were married in England that I went to visit my brother and his wife at their home in Liverpool. I found the first visit terribly difficult and would have avoided it if I could. Subsequent visits became easier and easier, until from becoming a duty they became a pleasure. Gradually as I got to know my sister-in-law, Protasia, I came to like her, then I came to love her and experienced her love for me. It was her love for me that effected the cure. It did for me what no earthly power could have done, but after all, love isn't an earthly power.

"To begin with, it was her love for my brother that uncovered the terrible racism that I had no idea was in me, but in the end it was that same love reaching out to me that cured it. Her love enabled me to see the terrible truth that I shrank from, and then it gave me the strength to rise above it. The strange thing is that when a loving relationship changes your attitude to one member of a group or tribe or race that you had been prejudiced against before then your attitude changes to every member of that group. It doesn't make you think they are all wonderful, but it does mean that you treat them according to their merit, not your prejudice.

"Some years ago I had to go to Africa to give a series of talks to different groups of people in Uganda, Kenya and Cameroon. I felt completely at home. Many of them remarked on the ease with which I was able to mix with everyone without the slightest hint of the patronizing way I had treated black Africans before. I have my sister-in-law, Protasia, to thank for that. That's what love can do. I don't mean to suggest that her love changed me completely, it didn't. I was still full of a hundred and one racial and other prejudices that I knew I would have to face up to one way or another if I was going to be the sort of open, balanced and Christ-like person that I ought to be. But what I learned from her was that love and love alone can change a blind and prejudiced bigot like me into the person I would like to be.

"I realized that it's not just love but the experience of being loved that frees a person from the prejudices that make so-called rational human beings behave irrationally towards one another. However, I could see that it was no good depending on chance encounters to purify me of the innumerable prejudices that I knew corrupted me from within. Only the Perfect Psychiatrist who was sent to the spiritually sick on the first Pentecost day could do that. Only He could show me the real truth about myself and give me the love that would empower me to rise above it.

"When I realized this I packed up teaching altogether and retired to the little island of Vatersay and later to Calvay in the Outer Hebrides, to find the place where I could radically open myself to the only One who could heal me from the inside. It was in that solitude that I had to undergo the baptism of fire in the dark night, where the Perfect Psychiatrist shows you the truth, the whole truth and nothing but the truth. It was here that I had to see not just my prejudices, but all the pride and the perverted love within me. I had to see the insufferable selfishness that had ruled my life so far, and which would continue to rule it if something, or rather if Someone, didn't do something about it.

"I saw quite clearly that although I'd been created in the image of the 'New Man,' the 'Old Man,' the egoist within me, had the power to destroy me if he were allowed to do it. His love was twisted, perverted. He loved everyone and everything, including God, for what he could get out of them. Even God-given impulses to give oneself in love to another, to have a home, to bring up one's own children and order one's life and family for the good of all, could be reduced to lust, greed and power-seeking. And then, if the egoist couldn't get what he wanted he'd be consumed with anger against those who stood in his way, and with envy and jealousy against anyone who had what he felt had been denied him. I saw all this and so much more as the Perfect Psychiatrist was working so that the 'New Man' could reign where the 'Old Man' had reigned before."

"I find what you're saying is frightening," I said, "at least it frightens me. I think what you call a Freudian slip was really a gift of God and it's led to more gifts, but I'm beginning to wonder if I want them. If all that you say is true — and I believe it is — it's true for me, too. I'm as blind as you ever were and as in need of the Perfect Psychiatrist as you were. But tell me, how does He show you the truth? Does He speak to you or show you visions or give you some sort of infused knowledge in prayer?"

"No! He doesn't do any of those things," said Peter. "He does only one thing. He just keeps on doing what He does all the time. He just keeps on loving. The purification begins to take place as you respond to His loving. To begin with, as you have found, it's difficult to turn to Him and open your heart to allow Him in because your heart's pulled in so many directions by temptations and distractions. They are but a pale reflection of the powerful perverted desires and urges that have been shut away below-stage in the unconscious. Then as you persevere, putting all the distractions under the cloud of forgetfulness and doing all in your power to keep your heart's attention on the cloud of unknowing and the One who is hidden behind it, a subtle change begins to take place. This subtle change is the first sign that the Perfect Psychiatrist is about to begin His work.

"There are no dramatics to begin with, in fact you hardly feel anything. It's just that you begin to notice over a period of time that, although you get nothing out of this strange new form of prayer without feelings, you are in some way impoverished without it. You get a subtle and hardly definable strength that you need to maintain some semblance of the Christian life to which you aspire. Then, when you least expect it, you begin to find yourself drawn into a sort of recollectedness that does not banish the distractions that disturbed you before but continues in spite of them. This experience comes and goes and is in no way dependent on your choosing. Then it can deepen and widen and become more and more absorbing. This is what Saint Teresa of Avila calls the Prayer of Recollection, as I explained to you before. At times the experience becomes more and more intense, raising you up into ever higher degrees of mystical awareness, into the Prayer of Quiet or even the Prayer of Full Union, when the absorption is so great that there are no longer any distractions or temptations at all.

"Now, as you become more and more absorbed in the love of God whose Spirit envelops you, you are, as it were, lifted up out of yourself and off the stage where you so often performed in the past. Then, as you are no longer able to keep your feet firmly on the trapdoor that you have always kept closed, it opens to admit what you've never admitted before. Gradually, the unacceptable works and pomps of the unconscious work their way up and on to the stage. When the temporary absorption of your will is discontinued and it returns, as it were, to its senses, then those senses have to see what they were always able to avoid seeing in the past. You have to see something of the truth about yourself, that you'd always tried to hide from before as well as keeping it from others.

"If you continue persevering in prayer, come what may, the subtle magnetic force of God's love becomes stronger and stronger, and draws more and more of the moral muck and mire out of your unconscious mind as it draws your conscious mind towards itself. So great highs are followed by great lows, light is followed by darkness. The experience of God's goodness is followed by the experience of one's own badness. Now the 'Old Man' is seen for what he is. He may well have been originally created in the image and likeness of the 'New Man,' but he has become twisted and perverted by what has traditionally been called original sin, the sin of others that is handed on to one generation after another by nature and nurture. He is not only affected by the 'sins of the fathers' through his genes, but by the sinfulness of his parents, brothers and sisters, friends and relatives, and others who project their sinfulness on to him by what they say and do and determine his growth for better or worse.

"Then personal sin adds to the influences that are brought to bear on him by the sins of others. All these powerful influences combine to pervert the love that should be directed towards God and the neighbor in need, and turn it inwards instead, where it festers as it loves itself. The 'Old Man,' the egotist, thrives on self love, he wants the world to revolve around him, he wants to take what he wants when he wants it and is consumed with anger when he is thwarted. It is the works and pomps of this egotist that everybody tries to hide from others, as they try to hide them from themselves, by shutting them away deep down below-stage in the unconscious. Only the power of God's love, the Holy Spirit, the Perfect Psychiatrist, who is both love and truth at one and the same time, can heal and make whole what cannot be healed without Him.

"It was once thought that a person could be healed from abnormal human behavior that prevented growth merely by unearthing the cause of that behavior in the unconscious and presenting it to the conscious mind. This was the half-baked idea that my psychology lecturer had taught at college. The theory was that once the cause of their abnormal behavior was seen and understood, then it would automatically facilitate the necessary healing and return to psychological health. Unfortunately it is not true; it is just a modern psychiatric representation of the old Socratic fallacy that knowledge is enough. Knowledge is not enough, something further is required. It is not enough just to see the truth, to see what has been preventing human growth, but it is necessary to experience simultaneously the love that enables that growth to continue. It was some time before it was fully realized that the psychotherapist's skill at unearthing the cause of abnormal behavior must be complemented by a loving kindness and compassion that is the main factor in facilitating the healing of the patient. This is what I learned for myself from the love I received from my sister-in-law, Protasia.

"A good and successful psychiatrist will always be characterized by an ability to uncover the truth while simultaneously imparting a genuine, healing love. However, the Perfect Psychiatrist will be able to uncover the whole truth and impart the fullness of love that will free a person, not just from some psychiatric obstacles that prevent them becoming normal human beings, but from all obstacles, both psychiatric and spiritual, that prevent them from becoming perfect human beings.

"My mother encountered the healing power of the Perfect Psychiatrist reaching out to her through the love of her husband and the love of her children. To begin with, her love for them enabled her to forget herself as she tried to live for them alone. But gradually, and precisely because her love was engaged elsewhere, she too lost control of the trapdoor that opened to allow what had been hidden below-stage to surface. Then she had to start seeing what she'd never seen before, and to face the sin and selfishness that would prevent her loving her husband and her children as fully as she would wish. She had to face the fear that what nature and nurture had done to her might be done to her children if she couldn't prevent it, and it didn't seem that she could. And so it was that the very love that drew her to her husband and to her children was the self-same love that began to draw out of her all that prevented the fullest possible union with them that she desired above all else. And she, like so many other married people, entered into her dark night without realizing it, to be purified from all that would prevent her from becoming the perfect wife and mother that she wanted to be.

"My father said to me that if divorce had been as easy in his day as it is in ours, he does not know if either he or my mother could have resisted the temptation to cut and run when their love was tested to the fullest in the darkest moments of the night. But it was precisely because they held on, come what may, and kept on giving and loving that their mutual love was deepened. So they ended up far more secure in each other's love than they had been when they started. Now the self-same purification that they experienced in their dark night has to be experienced in our dark night. It is here that the Perfect Psychiatrist works to destroy the evil 'Old Man' within, and purifies the inner desires and urges that have been twisted and perverted. It is here that He draws out all that festers in the depths, as the heat of a poultice draws all the impurities from a festering wound. This is how the Perfect Psychiatrist operates in the dark night to bring the mystic through into the light, putting to death the 'Old Man' so that he may be fitted into the 'New Man.' It is indeed a mystic death, that in some ways parallels physical death. I don't know if you've ever read Elisabeth Kübler-Ross?"

"No, I haven't," I said.

"She's a doctor," said Peter, "who has studied the various stages a person goes through in the dying process. I came across her by chance and was astounded by how closely these stages parallel the stages that a person has to go through in mystical death."

"What are they?" I said.

"She mentions five," said Peter. "Firstly denial and then anger, followed by bargaining that inevitably leads to depression and finally acceptance. At the beginning of their mystical death, a person whose experience of God seemed so vibrant and alive before can't or doesn't want to believe that they are on any sort of mystical journey, and will even try to convince their spiritual director that the diagnosis is wrong. But if they do nevertheless persevere and things get progressively worse, as I've indicated, then they become angry and like so many people who suffer from anger they begin to cope with it by projecting it on to others with whom they live or work. They can become very bad-tempered and bitter. Then they can turn on God, the so-called God of love who's got them into the mess in which they find themselves, who doesn't seem to care a fig, doesn't seem to be doing anything to get them out of it.

"And so in dark moments they can curse and blaspheme against God. Dr. Kübler-Ross shows how in a physical death a person bargains with God for the reversal of their sickness, promising to live the good and decent lives they didn't live before, promising anything to the only One who seems capable of doing what medical science seems incapable of doing. This is the only stage that has no parallel in mystical dying, because in mystical dying a person can choose to run away at any time, run away from the prayer life that enables the Perfect Psychiatrist to continue the purification that causes such spiritual and psychological pain.

"Depression sets in when anger seems to get them nowhere, and they have to face more and more the murk that is dragged up from the depths. It seems that they can do nothing about it, as they become ever more passive. When asked what he found most difficult in the spiritual journey, the Curé D'Ars said 'Depression.' No sinner can become a saint without having to pass through depression, depression far deeper than most of us have to face, because few of us ever have to face up to our real selves. Although the main work is done by the Holy Spirit, there is something that can be done to assist Him. When we see the sinners that we are, the sins that we have committed and the guilt that we have suppressed being hauled out into the full light of day, it's time for confession.

"The Desert Fathers always taught that one should seek out a holy person to whom one should open one's heart. Later it became more common to submit oneself to a priest in the sacrament of confession, to receive absolution and the psychological peace of mind that confession brings. However, it's not only one's sins that have to be seen and faced but the sins of others, too, that may have disfigured one physically or psychologically from childhood. It could be helpful to seek out a person with genuine psychological qualifications and expertise to help heal the scars from the past that can hinder one's journey in the present. When the darkness of depression becomes prolonged and debilitating, it may be appropriate to approach a doctor. Modern anti-depressants can be of great help, not only to alleviate the worst psychological effects of depression but also to restock certain chemical resources in the brain that are always depleted in depression. Depression has physical as well as psychological effects on the sufferer."

Peter took out a handkerchief and mopped his brow. I turned the gas fire down. It was getting quite hot and oppressive in the room.

"I'm sorry to sound like a prophet of doom," said Peter, "but I'm telling you the truth, not to put you off but to support you by preparing you in advance for what will most certainly happen if you choose to continue on the journey. Now, although therapists, counselors, doctors and such can be a great help in this journey, it is of paramount importance to have a good spiritual director if at all possible. Their role will be to oversee everything, otherwise the essential spiritual nature of the journey through depression can be lost sight of in its darkest moments.

"A person needs to be continually reminded of what is happening, because their faith in the love of God seems to evaporate at times. When a person no longer feels the love of God for prolonged periods of time they begin to say, 'Where is God?', and then 'There is no God,' and if there is no God there is no hope. And so the famous temptations come at last in the darkest moments — temptations against what are called the theological virtues, the very foundations of the spiritual life — temptations against faith, hope and charity.

"If there is no love, there is no hope; and so when a person's faith is put to the ultimate test they can even be tempted to take their lives, because what is the point of living without love? Remember Saint Thérèse of Lisieux warned her sisters not to leave poisonous medicine by her bedside when she was in her darkest hour. It is at the midnight hour in this dark night that a person experiences a truth that they thought they had known before, but which they had only known intellectually. It is that the desire for God is God's gift, and what He gives He can take back. Even though I said at the beginning that this desire for God is one of the first signs that a person is on the right path, even this is ultimately taken away for a time. So too are the theological virtues, faith, hope and love. They are God's gifts. What He gives He can take away, or at least it seems He takes them away, so that a person gradually learns not to take for granted what they had taken for granted before.

"Having said all this, I must say that great wisdom is learned in the dark night, though it seems that nothing is learned at all. There is much that is good as well as evil in the unconscious and this too is drawn out in the purification. Spiritual travelers rarely see it for themselves because they are all too conscious of the sinfulness that they have to come to terms with. But others see in them a wisdom that they cannot see, a wisdom that they have learned in their dark mystical purification. Others seek them out for help and advice that they give so accurately and with such compassion. All they can see, however, is their utter helplessness, their sinfulness and their weakness. For long periods of time it seems that they cannot pray at all. It seems that there is nothing spiritual in them. All they can do now is to wait patiently at the foot of the Cross. Although they do not realize it at the time, it is here that their prayer life is about to reach its highest point this side of the Mystical Marriage.

"If all they can manage to do at the darkest moments is to cry out 'help,' then it's a cry from the heart that reaches the heavens because it's the most powerful prayer they have ever made. The author of *The Cloud of Unknowing* said that this prayer is like the cry of a drowning man. When a man rises for the third time from the water that threatens to drown him, he doesn't waste a single breath on anything other than his deepest need and so he cries out 'help.' At that moment the drowning man is more totally one than ever before, body and soul, heart and mind, united in that single cry. The same is true of the mystic in their hour of greatest need, when they have waited and waited at the foot of the Cross, when they have learned patience the hard way, when they have learned true humility. Then, when they cry for help, they make the most powerful prayer that they have ever made.

"This is the moment when their heartfelt cry enables them to be raised up from the foot of the Cross to be united with the

Priestly Prayer of the One who hangs upon the Cross. They are now able to enter into the same Priestly Prayer that Christ made throughout His life, as it reaches its most perfect expression at the end of His life. It was a prayer that was made *in extremis* when surrounded by terrible sufferings and awesome temptations. It was a prayer in which He finally committed Himself to His Father with His whole heart and mind and being.

"The mystic is finally fitted into the 'New Man' at the moment when their priestly sacrifice is brought to its completion. Now they no longer even pray for help, as they pray not just in harmony with Christ but in total conformity with Him — 'Father, into your hands I commend my spirit.' This is the prayer of complete acceptance, the final stage of mystical death.

"Now, as they experience their own human weakness as never before, the mystic enters into the moment when Christ experienced His human weakness as never before. They enter into what the Greek Fathers called His *kenosis,* His self-emptying, so that they can be totally open in, with and through Him to what they call the *pleroma,* the fullness of the Father's life, the final and complete gift of the Holy Spirit. It is this gift which brought about the definitive *theosis,* the divinization, of Christ's human being and human acting. In the same way, it is this self-same gift who brings about the *theosis,* the divinization, of the 'Old Man' as he is transformed into the 'New Man' in the Mystical Marriage.

"This final transformation is instantaneous. The moment the baptism of fire has been completed in the dark night, the very second sin has been forgiven and its roots have been destroyed at source, is the moment when the mystic can receive the gift of the Holy Spirit. Then he can experience the peace that surpasses understanding as he is fitted fully into the 'New Man' who rose from the tomb on the first Easter Day."

Peter looked at his watch. "Dead on time," he said.

I looked at the clock on the mantelpiece. It was exactly one o'clock. Both of us stood up.

"I hope you don't mind," I said, "but I'm afraid I haven't prepared anything to eat. I'm hopeless at cooking, so I was thinking of taking you out for a meal."

"That's fine by me," said Peter. "I know the ideal place."

On our way there, I asked Peter how things worked out after his brother Tony had married Protasia.

"They worked out perfectly," said Peter. "Well, you could see for yourself. You met Protasia after the funeral, didn't you, and the two boys?"

"Yes, I did," I said. "They seemed to be a lovely family."

"Believe me, they are!" said Peter. "And yet I was one of many who were against the marriage and so was my brother David. But we were both wrong. I now believe that Tony made exactly the right decision. He's a changed person, thanks to Protasia's love, and I've already explained what her love did for me."

We parked the car outside Ye Olde Cock Inn where Peter had promised we could be sure of a good meal. He was right, and I needed it — it had been a long, hard morning, but I wouldn't have missed it for the world.

8

Peter didn't talk shop during the meal. Instead he told me something about the history of Didsbury, the village where he had been born. Apparently the pub in which we were having our meal had been a hotbed of mystery and intrigue at the time of the Jacobite Rebellion in 1745. The Young Pretender, Bonny Prince Charlie, had crossed the River Mersey near Didsbury on his way south and then again on his return when the hoped-for rising against the Hanoverians didn't materialize. A witch hunt followed in his wake, searching for the spies and sympathizers who'd supported the 'great enterprise' that reached its inglorious conclusion at Derby.

Many of them, for whom the pub, called The Bell in those days, had been a clandestine meeting place, had been executed on the village green. Peter told me that his interest in the Jacobite Rebellion revived when he spent a term teaching on the island of Eriskay, where he had lived in a crofter's cottage overlooking the beach on which the Bonny Prince had landed before sailing 'over the sea to Skye.'

We declined coffee at the pub and had it instead in the kitchen when we returned. I had it black. I wanted to be fully awake for what was going to be my last session with Peter before my departure.

"I found what you said about the psychology of purification fascinating," I said, "but I also found it frightening. I had no idea how penetrating and how painful it could be. No wonder so many people pack up prayer altogether when they begin to sense what is ahead of them. I almost feel like packing it in myself!"

"I understand your reaction," said Peter, "but I can't encourage you by playing down the truth, because if I did you'd underestimate what would be asked of you and eventually give up, like so many who are unprepared for the purification. If you only prepare a person for their expedition to the North Pole by waxing eloquent about the beauty of the scenery, the grandeur of the glaciers and the fascinating wildlife, then you leave them unprepared for the harsh realities ahead and so jeopardize the whole enterprise.

"They must be told the truth for their own good. They must be told that the temperature can fall to more than sixty degrees below zero, that they can lose limbs through frostbite, that glaciers can mean instant death and polar bears can attack on sight. Nevertheless, one must be prudent; sometimes it is better to explain the harshness of the journey ahead gradually, as the journey unfolds, because the early stages do help to harden the traveler for the ordeals ahead.

"What can be found and overcome with preparation and practice might never be overcome without it. That's why I usually only tell people about the sufferings involved in the baptism of fire gradually, as they approach them and experience them for themselves. I've made an exception in your case, because you are a priest to whom others will come for help and advice, so I feel that I should tell you the whole truth as far as I am able.

"Now is there anything else that you would like me to explain before I press on?"

"Well, yes," I said. "There are a few things I'd like to ask you about, if you don't mind. You see, whenever I really try to get to grips with someone like Saint John of the Cross I always get lost when they start speaking about visions, locutions and other strange phenomena that are quite beyond my experience."

"Yes," said Peter, "I know exactly what you mean. However, time is short and you are opening a very big subject, so let me be brief. When the baptism of fire begins in earnest you'll find you've never worked so hard before. The more the Holy Spirit draws out the evil that you yourself have done and the evil that has been done to you, the more depressed you become, and the more difficult it is to turn away from what you don't want to face to turn to the One you do. You become involved in a sort of spiritual tug-of-war that saps your energy. Add to this the sleepless nights that always accompany depression as it deepens, and you can easily be pushed to the extremes of exhaustion.

"Now once again depression is depression whatever its cause, and the features that are common to all depressions are also common to spiritual depression. In other words, a person can experience hallucinations that seem real. They can see and hear things in their imagination and in their minds that seem to come directly from God or the saints or from some other spiritual source. In fact they have nothing to do with the mystic way in itself, nor do they come from God, but from the deep depression that has enveloped them.

"If it is a sign of anything, it is a sign that they need medical as well as spiritual help. Often beginners who are genuinely on the mystic way get carried away, and allow pride to talk them out of the restraint that a good spiritual director should impose upon them. Then they begin to practice irresponsible fasting, abstinence and even physical mortifications, all of which will exacerbate their depression and the psychic phenomena that are misinterpreted as spiritual.

"Now, Saint John of the Cross was writing many years before Freud and the birth of psychiatry, so he was not able to express himself in language that would be easily intelligible to a modern reader, but his judgment was nevertheless right and his spiritual direction is as good today as it was in his day. Though he doesn't fully understand the reasons for the strange visions and locutions that some people experience in the night, he does make it quite clear that they have nothing to do with the essence of the mystic way and no spiritual significance should be placed on them whatsoever."

"Thanks," I said. "That does make sense to me."

"One last point before I move on," said Peter. "Any great psychological stress or strain can cause tension, and tensions can have psychosomatic consequences. So a person who experiences all the trauma and all the tensions of the spiritual tug-of-war that must be experienced in the dark night can develop physical symptoms, too.

"Some people have headaches, neckaches, backaches and some, like me, toothaches. Whenever I'm put under pressure my gums and my teeth start to ache all over and then I usually get an abscess. I think I've spent most of my dark night in the dentist's waiting-room! These physical aches and pains are all caused by the tensions that lead to depression, but all sorts of other illnesses, infections and inexplicable maladies can develop too, especially when a person is exhausted and run down."

"I do follow the logic of what you're saying," I said. "But does it really have to be so hard, and so painful for a person who simply wants to love God?"

"I'm afraid it does," said Peter. "You see, love doesn't just want to rejoice in the one who is loved, it wants to enter into them, to be one with them continually. A self-centered, sinful human being cannot be united with God until all that separates the two has been completely destroyed. The work of the Perfect Psychiatrist is to destroy sin and the effects of sin so that the union for which a person has yearned from the beginning of their spiritual journey can take place at the end of it.

"A person who is unprepared for the psychological and physical repercussions that this purification can have on the mind and on the body will inevitably turn back. The journey only becomes possible because it is the work of the Holy Spirit who supports, strengthens and consoles the believer even in the darkest moments, as Christ Himself had been consoled in His darkest moments in the desert and in Gethsemane. All has seemed black and bleak because I have been trying to describe the journey through the night in some sort of logical sequence, but God does not act according to human logic.

"At any moment, the same 'angel of consolation' that consoled Jesus can console us. At any time, God's Power can suddenly make itself felt at an hour when we least expect it. The One who says He comes like a thief in the night comes to us in our night. Sometimes His Presence is soft and gentle, sometimes it is strong and all-absorbing, and sometimes it is powerful beyond belief, raising a person up and out of themselves to experience God's love to shattering degrees of intensity. At one moment He is there, the next He seems to have gone. The believer has to learn that he is totally in God's hands, and He comes and goes at His will, not at ours, and purifies us in His way, never in ours.

"The Perfect Psychiatrist will have done His work when we are so perfectly purified that we no longer have any will of our own that does not want to be one with the will of Christ. Then we can be fitted fully into His Perfect Prayer, the perfect sacrifice that He made. Then we will be open as He was open to the fullness of life that possessed Him on the first Easter Day."

"Thank you, Peter," I said. "I do follow you, and I do see that all you say makes sense, no matter how hard it may seem. I suppose I was thinking it wasn't fair that a person who chooses to embrace a celibate life like you and me should have it so much harder than others."

"But we don't," said Peter. "Look at my mother's spiritual journey — was her purification any easier because she was married and had four children? I tell you it wasn't. As I said to you before, she had to face the fear that what nature and nurture had done to her might be transmitted to her children if she couldn't prevent it, and it didn't seem that she could. No wonder she got depressed, and no wonder that depression deepened with the exhaustion of looking after young children, of endless work and sleepless nights. No wonder her faith, hope and love were tested to the limits. This is how my mother was purified in the dark night that seemed to go on and on, year in year out, in her married life. When the honeymoon phase fizzled out, she had to go into a long, dark tunnel until she was all but middle-aged and the children were grown up. Call it a tunnel of love if you like. Yes, there was love there, and moments of great joy, too, that made it all possible, but there was much suffering as well, that made it possible for her children to inherit something of what she had received through her purification.

"I know it's easy to think that the grass is greener the other side of the fence, but make no mistake about it, marriage is no soft option. Suffering is always hard to bear, but it is even harder when you can see how much those you love suffer because of what's not been purified in you."

"Yes," I said. "That was a thoughtless thing for me to say. I think the truth of the matter is that we celibates have an easy life compared to all the hardships and sufferings that most married people have to endure on their journey together. It's all too easy for those of us who don't have all the responsibilities of marriage to misuse the freedom that our way of life gives us, to live for ourselves and just become self-centered old bachelors."

"Yes, I have to agree with you," said Peter. "If married people don't have enough time for themselves, then celibates can often have too much time for themselves and they can become thoroughly self-centered. When you think about it, it's a pretty fundamental fault when the whole of the spiritual journey is a journey from selfishness to selflessness. It's so easy for them to get stuck in a rut, in middle age or even before, that they never get out of.

"It nearly happened to my brother David a few years ago. He'd done very well for himself; he was hardly in his thirties when he was made the director of a residential retreat and conference center in London. All of a sudden he was his own boss. He had a suite of rooms to himself, his own car and as much money as he wanted, within reason. He became highly successful at his job, put the center on the map and made it pay for itself with plenty over, which wasn't supposed to be possible in those days. Anyway, it all went a little to his head. He became a clerical whizz-kid who was always dining out with the 'right people,' played golf several times a week, loved going to the theater and was regularly to be seen in the best seats at Covent Garden.

"Then all of a sudden everything went stale on him. He became unhappy with what he had because, deep down, he knew he was running away from what he really wanted. You see, he'd had a series of profound spiritual experiences when he was a young religious that guaranteed he'd never be happy again in his life doing anything other than searching for more of what he'd already received. He was already well advanced in spiritual adolescence when he went into religious life. Then it suddenly came to an abrupt end in the middle of his novitiate. One day it was fire, the next day it was ashes. He sought help from the novice master, from his spiritual director and from other visiting priests, but nobody could explain satisfactorily what had happened and how he should go on. The novice master said, 'Don't worry about it, we all go through that stage,' but he didn't seem to know anything about the next stage or how to get there.

"After about eighteen months, when he was in the middle of trying to get to grips with philosophy, something suddenly happened in the prayer that he had never given up. Although his first fervor didn't return, he began to experience a subtle pull that grew out of the void within him. Then one evening he suddenly felt himself spiraling upwards inside his head, as if drawn by some powerful magnetic force. He found himself utterly absorbed in God, without any of the distractions and temptations that had been torturing him before. Night after night he experienced this pull to varying degrees of intensity. Although he was reluctant to talk about what he was experiencing, he felt he needed help, but none of the priests to whom he turned understood what he was talking about, except one. Father Gabriel told him that although the experiences were undoubtedly authentic, he must be prepared for them to go as quickly as they had come, and that they might not return for many years, if ever!

"He sought from the library what he couldn't find anywhere else. It was here that he discovered Saint John of the Cross and read the signs that I mentioned to you earlier. They made sense of what had made no sense before. Saint John of the Cross became his guide and his mentor, together with Saint Teresa of Avila, whose *Interior Castle* explained the powerful mystical experiences that he had encountered in his prayer. After several months he discovered that what Father Gabriel had said was true. The experiences seemed to tail off, and instead of light he experienced only darkness again. He didn't know what was happening for many years to come, he didn't know it was the Perfect Psychiatrist at work, beginning the purification that soon became too much for him. Had he received help he might have continued, but he didn't, and other pressures meant that he had to run away from what he would have to face one day in the future.

"Although there was always a deep restlessness within him, a nostalgia to return to what he'd experienced in the past, the excitement of his first years as a priest meant that he was constantly kept away from the prayer to which he knew he ought to return. The appointment as director of the retreat center only exacerbated his busyness, and the sense of intoxication he had from doing everything so successfully went to his head and would have been his total undoing if it hadn't been for what had been done in him ten or more years before.

"Although he studiously avoided the solitude that would have brought him to his senses, the Finger that had touched him before touched him again, not in the church but in the concert hall. It was in the beauty of the music that he loved so much that he began to experience the pull to return to the place where he'd experienced that pull before. It was then that he came out to visit me at my home on Barra and was amazed that my spiritual journey had been so similar to his own in those early years. Of course, we'd met at home in the intervening years but he was always so full of himself, of his achievements, of his sophisticated friends, that he never had time to enquire about me and my way of life. But now that had all changed, thanks to Mozart, Beethoven and Brahms. He was fascinated to find that I'd traveled on beyond the point of his departure from the mystic way. All of a sudden, I found myself in the strange position of acting as spiritual director to my own brother, who was eager to listen to all I had to say to help him return to the journey he had forsaken all those years before.

"I explained to him much of what I've explained to you, to help him practice the prayer of the heart. At first he found it very difficult and turned to the music that had already triggered off his 'second conversion' to turn his heart back to the One he had neglected for all too long. He found that the music not only created a pleasant environment in which to pray, but it positively helped to draw him together, and then reach out to the source of all beauty, all goodness and all truth. In time he found that even the music that had helped him had to be abandoned, as he was able to abandon himself to the subtle magnetic power that became stronger and stronger.

"The mystical experiences that had disappeared from his spiritual life many years before returned with even greater power and force. And so David's purification began in earnest, as the magnetic pull of God's love drew out wave after wave of all that needed to be cleansed from within him. For years he experienced presence then absence, light then darkness, death then resurrection, as the heart that was restless, and would remain restless until it rested in God, was gradually purified."

"And what happened next, when his purification was completed?" I said.

"That I can't tell you," said Peter, "because David's purification is far from finished. Ask him in ten years or more — who knows?"

Peter was smiling, but I didn't respond. I was too busy thinking of myself and the length of the painful journey ahead of me that I had hardly begun.

"But it seems a terribly long time for David to wait before he can be purified and prepared to help others," I said.

There was more than a touch of anger in my voice. I was protesting as much for myself as for David, in fact more so, and Peter knew it.

"Please," said Peter, "please don't misunderstand me. I'm not suggesting that only those who have scaled the heights can help those still fumbling around in the foothills. If that were true, what hope would there be for any of us? David may well have a long way to go, but he's already traveled further than he realizes and is worth ten times the arrogant know-it-all that he was before re-entering the night. Just what was he doing for others anyway, but giving scandal when he should have been giving example? He's the first to admit that most of his pastoral work was more to do with pursuing his own ends and his own needs than meeting the needs of the people he was supposed to be serving.

"The night has not yet made David into the man he is meant to be, but he is far closer than he ever was before. He's already had to see enough about himself that he'd never seen in the past to give him a measure of the humility that he only simulated before. When the night forced him to focus his entire attention upon God, or on what prevented him from doing so, he began to lose concentration on everything else that he had once thought so important. His memory continually let him down, so whenever he tried to play the part that he played so well before he was proved wrong, with such regularity that he simply had to stop pontificating. He became more tolerant of the faults and failings of others, too, when he had to face his own. His own inner sufferings made him feel for others whose sufferings he wouldn't even have noticed before. Although he was very far from being perfect, at least something of the goodness of the Man he wished to follow could be seen in him, and seen growing year by year. More and more people turned to him for the sort of advice that he couldn't possibly have given in the past. He began to see the truth in his darkness, not just about himself but about the spiritual life that he'd lost sight of amidst all his secular 'successes.'

"Then he began to preach about it, loud and clear, whether it was welcome or unwelcome. While many loved him for what he said, others hated him and wanted to destroy him, as they had destroyed the Man whose message he was trying to preach. All this was a blow to his security that received a further shock when our father phoned him to tell him the source of all his security had died."

Peter lapsed into silence for a few moments. He had so many things on his mind.

"I'm sorry, so sorry," he said. "I've overindulged myself again, but I was just trying to show how the night doesn't mean that a person becomes spiritually impotent until some sort of resurrection takes place in the distant future — far from it. David is many times the man he was when he thought the world was his for the changing, and he'll be many more times the man he is now when his journey reaches its completion. At the moment he thinks he's quite incapable of prayer, but if he can only try to accept what appears to be unacceptable he'll be praying more perfectly than he felt he prayed in any of the mystical experiences that enveloped him in the past.

"Although it seems he has no heart for anything any more, his heart is in fact being purified now, at this midnight hour of everything that seemed important to him in the past, so that in the future it will be much purer and much sharper to pierce the cloud of unknowing. Once breached by the prayer of a pure heart, the cloud can be breached again and again to admit the Perfect Psychiatrist, until His baptism of fire makes another home humble enough for His habitation."

Once again Peter fell into silence, this time gazing into the middle distance, miles away from what he'd been talking about the moment before. I knew I was being selfish, but I'd have to leave before the hour was up and there were still things I wanted to ask. It might be my last opportunity.

"So as the cloud is breached," I said, "or rather, as the dawn draws nearer, the pain of purification presumably becomes less and less?"

"Sorry?" said Peter.

He hadn't heard a word I said, so I repeated myself.

"Yes, I suppose that's true," he said, pulling himself together,

113

"but there's another pain that grows as the pain of purification pales. It's the pain of the pursuer who is denied what their heart yearns for more than anything else. As the deer yearns for running streams, as the dry, weary land pines for water, so the pursuer pines for the only One who can quench their thirst, and they feel frustrated, annoyed and angry whenever they're denied. The Desert Fathers used to say that anger is the last of the evil spirits to be cast out of the monk before he can attain peace of mind. It is this anger that shocks the believer who has already traveled far on the mystic way, when it suddenly bursts into flame and rages against whatever or whoever prevents them from enjoying the promised peace for which their whole being craves.

"They suffer, not just in their hearts but in their heads. They feel as if they will break into fragments if they can't return immediately to solitude, to prayer, to the pool of contemplative stillness that is their only solace. These sufferings only come to an end when the purification is finally finished."

"And what exactly does God do to bring this purification to an end?" I said.

"Once again, I have to say that He doesn't do anything that He hasn't been doing all the time," said Peter. "God is love, God is loving. The Transforming Union or the Mystical Marriage doesn't suddenly begin because God does something other than what He's been doing all along — it begins because what He's been doing all along finally destroys everything in us that's been keeping Him out. His love is only able to do this because we have been repeatedly turning to receive it, continually practicing repentance through the prayer of the heart. What was called Purifying Love during the night can be called Transforming Love at the end of it, not because it changes in itself, but because it changes what is in us. It has been at work throughout the night helping you to practice the most important virtue of all, selflessness, that will enable you to offer the only sacrifice that God really wants, the sacrifice of a pure and open heart.

"When you try to practice this virtue, you are in fact practicing the three most important virtues of all at one and the same time, what are traditionally known as the theological virtues. When you selflessly try to love Someone whom you cannot see or feel or touch, you are exercising the spiritual muscles of your mind that will generate a faith strong enough to move more than mere mountains. And when you try to love that Someone to the exclusion of all else, even though you seem to receive nothing in return, you are exercising the muscles of your heart as never before. Then that heart can learn how to love beyond all human loving, and hope beyond hope, until it receives much more than it ever hoped for.

"All the other moral virtues, like temperance and fortitude, that you can read about in the textbooks, are practiced repeatedly whenever you practice pure, selfless loving. In other words, you are practicing fortitude when you have to go on living and seem to be receiving nothing in return. You are practicing temperance too, that doesn't come easily to a self-indulgent human being, who'd far rather be sitting in front of the telly, or drinking in the pub, or dining at the club. These and all the moral virtues are practiced automatically as the supreme sacrifice of selflessness is continually offered to God through the prayer of the heart. It's rather like an athlete who brings his whole body to peak perfection by working with weights in the gym. Each time he raises the weights he is exercising not just the muscles in his arms but the muscles in every part of his body simultaneously.

"If vices are bad habits then virtues are good habits, that have to be learned and then brought to peak perfection by being exercised in the night, as the spiritual athlete raises his heart time and time again through the prayer of the heart. As the heart is repeatedly raised and opened to the action of the Holy Spirit then He is able to penetrate it, and percolate through into the whole person, to facilitate the process of forming the 'New Man' out of the 'Old Man.'

"Although the Holy Spirit is at work throughout the whole process, He works most perfectly at the end of it when, all obstacles removed, He can transform and perfect what was only imperfect before. He's like the master sculptor, who'd always have scores of apprentices to help him create his masterpieces. They would do the initial donkey-work on the roughly hewn figure under his guidance and inspiration. When they had done all they could do, then he himself would take over and with the delicate and deft touch of the master craftsman bring their imperfect work to perfection. This is how the Holy Spirit works with us and through us in the night, to act on the 'Old Man' so that he can be transformed into the 'New Man' at the end of it. This is the way He brings all virtues to peak perfection, so that the 'New Man' can act like the Perfect Man, Jesus Christ, in whose image and likeness man was first conceived and into whom he is gradually transformed. But He does even more, He gives gifts that were never given so fully before, so that the 'New Man' can mirror the Perfect Man.

"Just as the seven colors of the spectrum are sheathed within a single ray of light, so the seven gifts of the Holy Spirit are sheathed within a single ray of His love that penetrates the 'New Man.' The purified heart acts like a sort of spiritual prism that separates what is but one in God into different gifts in man, as the divine enters and is transposed into the human. For what is pure love in God is called the gift of knowledge by man, as it gives him an intuitive ability to penetrate human and divine truths without the labor of learning, or the strenuous effort that was needed to practice the virtues. This and the other gifts are always readily seen to an outstanding degree in the lives of the saints, who may be so devoid of human learning that they cannot even read or write, yet are possessed by a wisdom before which the great minds of their day can only prostrate themselves.

"In the night, the ray of divine light brought darkness; in the Transforming Union it brings brightness. A mind that was dull and clumsy before becomes clear and sharp. A heart that was hard and intractable becomes soft and malleable, and a body that had become slow and slovenly becomes active and alert to do what had become impossible in the night. Although much was done in the darkness for the searcher and for those whom they tried to serve, so much more is done now, as the divine is transposed into the human, so that yet another incarnation can take place to the glory of God and for the service of mankind. Whereas in the night, apart from the spiritual betrothals, the action of the Holy Spirit could only be experienced at brief moments in the mind or in the higher part of the head, it is experienced in the whole body in the Transforming Union as the divine life seeps ever deeper into the human.

"The feelings and the emotions that seemed to have frozen over in the night, as if in some strange spiritual ice age, return as the fire of the Holy Spirit thaws them out to move and act as they did at the outset of the mystic way. But now they have been purified, they are no longer at the mercy of passing whims, trivial sentimentality or the superficial and self-generated emotionalism that often characterizes spiritual adolescence. Now they have been refined to work in perfect harmony with the purified heart and mind of the 'New Man,' who is in some mysterious but very real way a genuine reincarnation of the Perfect Man. This is why I think I prefer the expression 'the Mystical Marriage' to 'the Spiritual Marriage,' because the latter can mistakenly give the impression that the union is of the mind only or of the higher spiritual faculties, whereas it is a union of persons, body and spirit, a union of personalities, of the divine with the human.

"As this interpenetration takes place and deepens, it gives back such security to those who had become so insecure in the night that they feel like new creatures, like butterflies who have emerged from a chrysalis, as Saint Teresa put it. Only love gives a person the security that they need, only love makes them free, free of all the insecurities that have stifled their human growth from the earliest years. No wonder there is so much joy for those who had thought that they had become unlovable, as they experience the continual and abiding presence of God's love enveloping their whole being. When Mother Teresa of Calcutta was asked what gave her such deep inner peace and security, she answered simply, 'The certain knowledge that nobody can separate me from the love of God.' It is this certain knowledge that is the continual companion of the believer who has entered fully into the Mystical Marriage.

"The lives of the saints give one example after another of how a man or a woman who has been transformed by the indwelling Spirit can do more for others in a matter of hours than an unpurified person can do in a lifetime. In them you can see the impossible made possible for the sake of God and His Kingdom, which is all that they want to live for in the future.

"It does not mean an end to suffering, but it gives a new meaning to suffering that is quite unintelligible for those of us who are still dragging our heels in the foothills. The suffering that they once reluctantly endured is now embraced and welcomed — it actually becomes their joy, because it becomes a means of expressing the love that they experience for God and for others, with whom they wish to share it. It enables them to do for others, even those whom they may never meet or never see, something of what has been done for themselves. If their own hearts became like prisms that enabled God's gift to be channeled into their whole beings, now their whole beings can become the prisms that enable that same love to be channeled to the world. And what they come to see is that the more the prism is one with Christ, and Christ crucified, then the more effective it becomes to channel to others what they have received from Him."

"Have you ever met anyone who has traveled through and beyond the night into the Transforming Union?" I said.

"Yes, of course," said Peter. "That's why I'm here now, to celebrate such a person's life — my own mother's. But I must admit I've found it very difficult. I just can't get over my own feelings of personal loss. I know it's all very selfish of me, but I simply can't help myself. Whenever I'm alone I just keep bursting into tears. I can't seem to help myself."

"But that's only natural," I said. "I know it's the in thing to talk about celebrating a person's life when they die, but when they're so close to you no talk of celebration can take away the terrible sense of loss, nor should it."

"I know," said Peter. "I know I really don't feel in the mood to celebrate anything, not even my own mother's life. The best I can do is to thank God for it and for all I've received from it. My job now is to try and support my father as best I can — he's totally bereft. You see, they were so close...."

Peter wanted to continue, but he couldn't. Once again he paused, and put his head in his hands. When he took them away to reach for his handkerchief I could see the tears in his eyes.

"You know," he said, as he put his handkerchief away, "when I came over to the mainland for a hospital appointment during the Edinburgh Festival, a friend took me to see *Tristan und Isolde* before I returned to Calvay, and I was so deeply moved that I cried through most of it. Is there anything in the whole realm of music, art or poetry that surpasses such sublime expressions of love as that ravishing duet in the second act? Their love was so strong, so vibrant, so full of feeling and passion that they couldn't bear to think of any form of separation. They would have preferred death together rather than life apart. At one point Tristan actually calls Isolde Tristan, and she calls him Isolde. They felt so completely as one that they didn't want any other identity than the identity they had in each other. They only became fully alive in the ecstasy of a love that lifted them out of themselves to find their fullest human completion in each other.

"I couldn't help thinking of my mother and father, and of the love that they had for each other that enabled them to travel on and on until they fully found themselves in each other in a quality of love that completely surpassed their understanding. Of course, Tristan and Isolde were young, and so was the love they bore for one another. They thought they had attained the height but it was, if they had only known it, only the beginning. But even in the beginning, their love was so strong that it enabled them to glimpse, in some way, something of the heights to which love is designed to lead two lovers. Their oneness was still all in the desire.

Much, much more has to happen before two lovers can be one in heart and mind and in body and soul.

"Although my mother was not a Wagnerian, she loved *Tristan und Isolde,* but her first and last love was Mozart, and her favorite opera was *The Magic Flute.* Once again it was the story of two lovers, Tamino and Pamina, that enthralled her. But this time the story didn't end with sublime expressions of mutual love. It went on, to show the trials that they had to endure, first alone and then together, as they journeyed on towards perfect love. Through one profound symbol after another, the nature of their dark night is expressed in words and music that were deeply impressed on my mother's memory. It was for her the most perfect artistic expression of the journey she had traveled with my father. My brother Tony bought her a videotape of Bergman's version of the opera for her seventieth birthday. I can't describe the joy it gave her. It was as if someone had said, 'This is your life,' in sign and symbol, in poetic picture-language and in verse, and most of all in some of the most exquisite and divine music that has ever been written. She loved watching the trials that the two lovers had to undergo, the baptisms of fire and water preceding their final victory, which would have been impossible without an other-worldly help and strength that was symbolized by the magic flute. The love that was generated and then deepened by their testing purification enabled them to receive the true wisdom that they could then share with their own future families, and other families who would look to them for help and inspiration.

"The opera meant so much to her that my father and I watched it together on Tuesday night. When it was over, he kept saying, as if to himself, 'I can't believe it, I can't believe it — it's all over now — it's all over now.' Despite how I felt myself, I tried to tell him that it wasn't over, it was just a new beginning, a new phase in the purification that would one day bond them together more closely than ever before. Our destiny is not just to go out of ourselves into love but to go out of ourselves again and again, for there is no end to the journey into the infinite sea of love into which we all desire to plunge ourselves.

"The reward of the traveler is to go on traveling, the solace of the searcher is to go on searching. My parents' journey has not ended, it is on the verge of a new beginning for which they are both being prepared by a short but painful separation. Once they are reunited they will never be separated again, nor will their journey end this side of eternity.

"But unfortunately we live in time," said Peter, looking at his watch, "and I'm afraid it's time you should be on your way if you want to get home this side of midnight. Let's see if we can find something in the kitchen to see you on your way."

Peter put a loaf on the table and began looking in vain for a bread knife, while I raided the fridge and scattered all the week's leftovers before us. I was just thinking how I would have loved to have met Peter's mother. I desperately wanted to meet someone who had in some way lived and then embodied the ideals that Peter had been speaking about. I knew it was a rather adolescent whim, but after all I was just an adolescent, at least a spiritual adolescent, and adolescents can't help wanting role models, can't help wanting to see the ideals to which they aspire embodied in someone they can look up to and admire. We all need that sort of inspiration from time to time.

"Bread?" said Peter.

"Yes, please," I said.

"Are you all right?"

"Yes, sorry, I was just daydreaming," I said, and then it happened.

As Peter took the bread and broke it, I saw him as I'd never seen him before. I saw him as the living embodiment of the Man I wanted to be, and I felt privileged to be sharing a meal with him, as Christ Himself had shared a meal with His disciples on the road to Emmaus. Like them, my heart had been burning within me all the time as Peter had explained to me how it was only to be expected that Christ would have to suffer in order to enter into His glory, as would those who would follow Him.

I offered him my hand as I left. He took it in both of his and gazed on me with eyes full of compassion, but he said nothing. Everything had been said that needed to be said, at least for the present. I drove away as if in a dream, as if I was inebriated by what Peter had given me at our parting, though no word had passed his lips. It was as if I were under the influence of some powerful, elevating drug that enveloped my whole being. His touch had communicated to me in some small way, for some short time, what he experienced in a far greater way all the time. Of that I was quite certain. I knew that what he had given me would soon fade away, for I could not sustain it.

I was so lost in all that had happened to me over the past week, and most of all over the past day, that I didn't notice the car that came abreast of me on the motorway. I didn't notice the red fluorescent stripe, the flashing blue light or the man with the face of granite at the wheel — that is until he tooted his horn. This time the face of granite cracked into the semblance of a smile and invited, not ordered, me to turn on to the hard shoulder.

"So sorry to stop you again," he said, "but I just wanted to ask about Peter and his family. I had no idea whose funeral it was that I was taking you to until I got home that evening. My wife had been there and was deeply moved. Of course, the name Peter Calvay didn't mean anything to me at all until my wife told me whose funeral it was. I used to go to school with Peter years ago. Our families have known one another for over thirty years."

I told him all I could. I said a few cliches about time being the great healer — I hadn't anything else to say. I was still lost in the dream world that he had just interrupted.

"You know," he said, "that family has done more for me and my family than any other I know, not by anything that they've said, or anything that they've done, but by being what they are. I can't tell you how much I owe them."

"Well, I can tell you this," I said. "They've done more for me in a matter of days than years of theology have ever done for me!"

As I drove past him he lowered his window and gave me a knowing look.

"Mind how you go," he said.

"Oh, don't worry about me," I said. "I can assure you, from now on I'm moving out of the fast lane for good."